S0-AAA-846

Geography
SIMULATIONS

Written by Max W. Fischer

Illustrated by Kathy Bruce

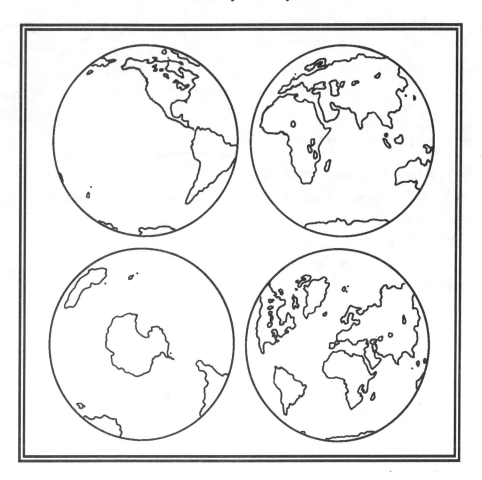

Teacher Created Materials, Inc.
P.O. Box 1040
Huntington Beach, CA 92647
©1995 Teacher Created Materials, Inc.
Made in U.S.A.

ISBN 1-55734-483-3

The classroom teacher may reproduce copies of materials in this book for classroom use only. The reproduction of any part for an entire school or school system is strictly prohibited. No part of this publication may be transmitted, stored, or recorded in any form without written permission from the publisher.

Table of Contents

Introduction

Contemporary surveys have made us aware that many students lack geographic knowledge. When a percentage of high school seniors believes Vietnam is the nation directly south of the United States, one knows there is work to be done.

Perhaps educators need to move away from traditional, passive methods of instruction and towards a more interactive approach. *Geography Simulations* is written from such a belief: namely, that pupils must be actively involved, obtaining knowledge through cognitive, affective, or kinesthetic approaches to learning.

In ***Section I: Map Skills — Physical and Political Features*** simulations, simulated review games, and problem–solving dilemmas are used to employ the use of map skills and enhance understanding of the physical and political features of our world. However, a clear understanding of political and physical features of geography is not sufficient in itself. Thus, ***Section II: Humanity and the Environment*** provides simulations, situations, and activities that demonstrate how humans interact with the geographic environment, placing students squarely at the center of active situations that call for participation. Furthermore, ***Section III: Regional Interaction***, involves students in critical thinking, enabling them to identify some of the interconnecting relationships that exist among the peoples of the planet.

By making optimal use of a cooperative learning environment, *Geography Simulations* will help middle school students think of geography as an adventure rather than work. Through action and participation, the knowledge students are exposed to will be internalized. Simulations make the learning process more natural and enjoyable and give results that last longer than those achieved with rote memorization.

Success with Simulations

The activities in *Geography Simulations* have been selected in order to get students affectively involved with geography by simulating conditions of a particular geographical area within the limited confines of the school environment.

Whether you intend to use a simulation for the purposes of introduction, review, or as part of the closure process, it is wise to establish procedures throughout each unit that will maintain consistency and organization. Suggestions on how best to utilize and store the units in this book follow.

Simulation Format

Each simulation begins with a lesson plan designed to assist the teacher with the preparations and procedures necessary and closes with valuable background information which connects the simulation to the geographical conditions being studied. The lesson plan for each simulation follows this format:

> - Title of Simulation
> - Topic
> - Objective
> - Materials
> - Preparation
> - Procedure
> - For Discussion (where applicable)
> - Background (where applicable)
> - Follow-Up (where applicable)

Storing Simulations

As you use each activity, you will want to save the components of the simulation by using a readily available and well-organized system which will serve the future as well as the present. Labeled file folders or large manila envelopes can be easily sorted and organized by simulation units and kept in a file box. Pages that will be duplicated or made into overhead transparencies can be stored in the file folders or envelopes. Game cards, labels, etc., should be placed in envelopes or resealable plastic bags before storing them in their respective folders. If possible, use index paper or heavy stock for reproduced items, such as game pieces, that will be used over and over again. Lamination will help preserve these items.

Outside materials such as candy or plastic spoons should be readily available and noted on the outside of the activity's folder to serve as a reminder that these items need to be accessible for the simulation.

Once the simulations have been organized into a file box, you will be prepared for each unit on a moment's notice.

Let the simulations begin!

Cooperative Learning Teams

Cooperative learning is an important instructional strategy because it can be used as an integral part of many educational processes. It is made-to-order for thinking activities. It acts as a powerful motivational tool.

Many of the activities in this unit involve the cooperative learning process in order to find solutions or come to conclusions regarding the simulations. With this in mind, consider the following information as you initiate team activities.

Four Basic Components of Cooperative Learning

1. **In cooperative learning, all group members need to work together to accomplish the task.** No one is finished until the whole group is finished and/or has come to consensus. The task or activity needs to be designed so that members are not simply completing their own parts but are working to complete one product together.

2. **Cooperative learning groups should be heterogeneous.** It is helpful to start by organizing groups so that there is a balance of abilities within and among groups. Some of the simulations in this book, however, require a specific type of grouping for cooperative teams in order to achieve the simulation objective. Under such circumstances, a balanced and heterogeneous cooperative learning team arrangement would not be appropriate for the success of the simulation.

3. **Cooperative learning activities need to be designed so that each student contributes to the group, and individual group members can be assessed on their performance.** This can be accomplished by assigning each member a role that is essential to the completion of the task or activity. When input must be gathered from all members of the group, no one can go along for a free ride.

4. **Cooperative learning teams need to know the social as well as the academic objectives of a lesson.** Students need to know what they are expected to learn and how they are supposed to be working together to accomplish the learning. Students need to process or think and talk about how they worked on social skills as well as to evaluate how well their group worked on accomplishing the academic objective. Social skills are not something that students automatically know; these skills need to be taught.

SIMULATION #1

The Continent of West Podiatry

Topic

Landform features and the use of map scale

Objective

Students will identify more than one dozen geographic terms pertinent to physical features found on a map. They will calculate distances between locations on a map using map scale.

Materials

- overhead projector
- pages 8 and 9, reproduced (one copy for each student)
- overhead transparencies of pages 9 and 10

Preparation

1. Prepare overhead transparencies of West Podiatry maps.
2. Reproduce copies of pages 8 and 9 for students.
3. Obtain and ready an overhead projector.

Procedure

1. Discuss or review primary landform terminology, then display the transparency of page 9 (map with locations numbered) on the overhead and hand out copies of page 9.

2. While the transparency is on view, students can work individually or in cooperative teams to label the map features on their copies of the map, matching geographically named features with the numbered locations on the map.

3. The transparency of page 10 can be used for correction and discussion of geographic features after students have completed page 9.

4. After page 9 has been completed, hand out page 8 for students to complete. The answers to pages 8 and 9 are shown on page 7.

The Continent of West Podiatry

(cont.)

Background

"West Podiatry" attempts to mix a bit of humor into what is often considered an extremely dry subject. Once students are successful at identifying geographic features on this imaginary continent, they should be able to recognize similar geographic features and use scales on other maps.

— Answer Key —

Page 8

Map Scale

1. 4,500 miles
2. 1,200 miles
3. 900 miles
4. 3,600 miles
5. 900 miles
6. C
7. B
8. B
9. A
10. A

Page 9

Matching

6	North Foot Ocean
13	South Foot Ocean
8	Mt. Crackatoa
7	Corn Mountain Range
10	Blister Lake
11	Blister Delta
16	Bunion Strait
3	Gulf of Fallen Arches
14	Isthmus of Lint
2	Little Toe River
17	Blister River
9	Second Digit Peninsula
5	West Itch Bay
4	East Itch Bay
1	Big Toe Island
12	Cape Hangnail
15	Callus Hills
18	East Podiatry

Using Map Skills

Directions: Complete the map on page 9. Use the map to answer the following questions.

Map Scale Questions

1. What is the length of West Podiatry from north to south? _____

2. What is the distance from Mt. Crackatoa to the mouth of the Little Toe River? _____

3. What is the length of the Little Toe River? _____

4. What is the distance from Big Toe Island to the Isthmus of Tootsies? _____

5. How far is it from Cape Hangnail to Mt. Crackatoa? _____

Multiple Choice *(Circle the answer.)*

6. At its widest point, how wide is West Podiatry from east to west?

   A. 1,200 miles   C. 1,800 miles

   B. 2,400 miles   D. 700 miles

7. How long is the Corn Mountain Range?

   A. 4,200 miles   C. 2,100 miles

   B. 1,500 miles   D. 900 miles

8. How long is the Blister River from its source to its delta?

   A. 700 miles   C. 1,200 miles

   B. 300 miles   D. 100 miles

9. What is the approximate distance from east to west across the Isthmus of Lint?

   A. 150 miles   C. 50 miles

   B. 300 miles   D. 600 miles

10. At its longest point from north to south, what is the distance of the Gulf of Fallen Arches from Bunion Strait to the Isthmus of Lint?

    A. 3,150 miles   C. 5,400 miles

    B. 4,000 miles   D. 2,400 miles

Numbered Map of West Podiatry

Student Directions: Match each of the numbered physical features with one of the place names listed below.

_____ North Foot Ocean

_____ South Foot Ocean

_____ Mt. Crackatoa

_____ Corn Mountain Range

_____ Blister Lake

_____ Blister Delta

_____ Bunion Strait

_____ Gulf of Fallen Arches

_____ Isthmus of Lint

_____ Little Toe River

_____ Blister River

_____ Second Digit Peninsula

_____ West Itch Bay

_____ East Itch Bay

_____ Big Toe Island

_____ Cape Hangnail

_____ Callus Hills

_____ East Podiatry

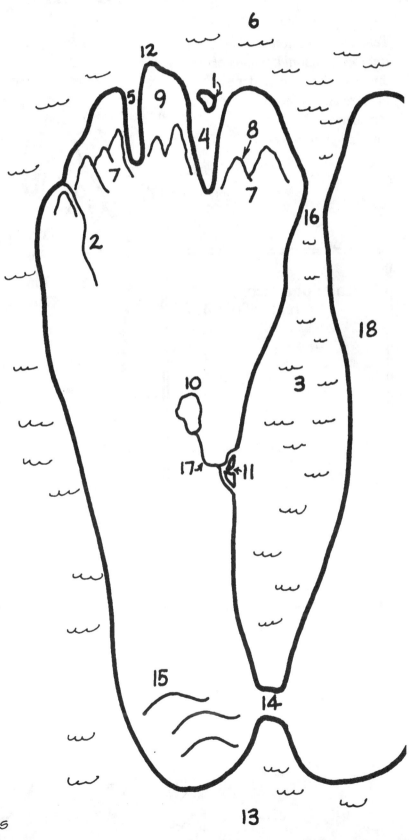

Scale: One inch equals 600 miles

Labeled Features Map of West Podiatry

Teacher Directions:
Reproduce enough copies of this page for each student. Prepare an overhead transparency for the simulation on pages 9-10.

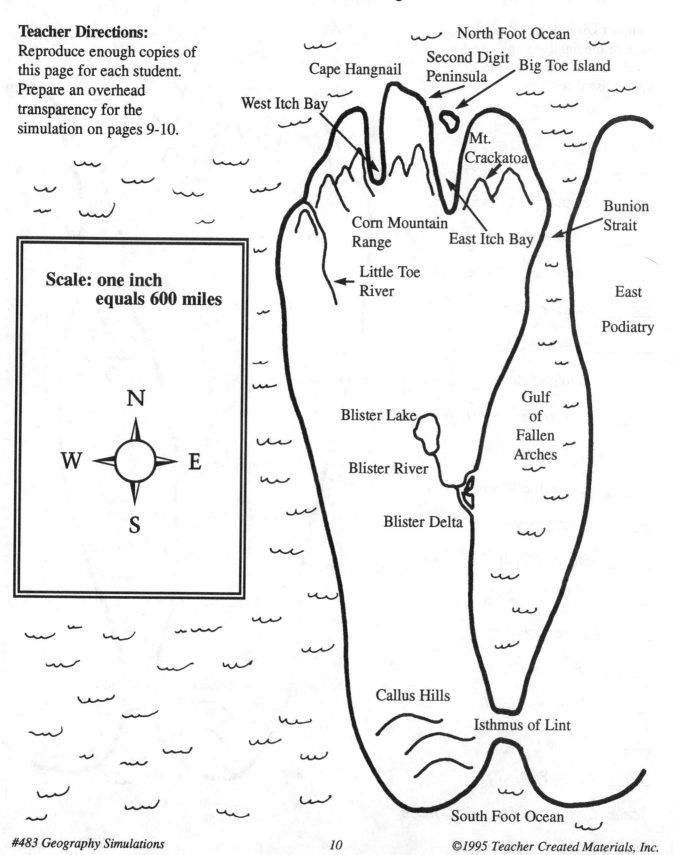

Scale: one inch
equals 600 miles

North Foot Ocean

Cape Hangnail

Second Digit Peninsula

Big Toe Island

West Itch Bay

Mt. Crackatoa

Bunion Strait

Corn Mountain Range

East Itch Bay

East Podiatry

Little Toe River

Gulf of Fallen Arches

Blister Lake

Blister River

Blister Delta

Callus Hills

Isthmus of Lint

South Foot Ocean

Direction March

Topic

Cardinal and intermediate directions

Objective

Students will move toward a designated cardinal or intermediate direction as instructed by a game card.

Materials

- overhead projector
- overhead transparency of page 14
- several small game markers such as buttons to use on the overhead with page 14
- pages 12–13, reproduced on heavy stock paper

Preparation

1. Copy, cut, and shuffle direction cards.
2. Make a transparency of the game board or draw it on the chalkboard.
3. Obtain game markers.

Procedure

1. Students may play the game as individuals or as teams, depending upon teacher preference.
2. Place the game board transparency on the overhead so that it is readily visible to all students.
3. For each team or individual playing, place a game marker on one of the four lines touching the "START" point.
4. The teacher (or other designated direction "caller") turns over one direction card for each player or team and announces the move, for example, "3 Spaces West."
5. Using the overhead transparency, the individual or designated team member must then move his or her marker the appropriate direction and distance along the interconnecting lines and points—vertically (N-S), horizontally (E-W), or diagonally (NE-SW, NW-SE).
6. Once the player releases the marker, his or her turn is over and the caller proceeds to the next team.
7. Players cannot exit the board on moves that would pass through the arrow points.
8. The game may be played so that either the first team (player) or the last team (player) to exit the board is the winner. With respect to incorrect responses, if the goal is to exit first, incorrect moves dictate that the marker be returned to "START." However, if the object is to be the last to leave the board, incorrect answers will cause that marker to be placed on a point at the edge of the board (not on an arrow point).

Background

"Direction March" is primarily designed for students with little experience in map reading skills and are having difficulty mastering the intermediate directions. Depending upon the experience of the students involved, the instructor may want to include a simple compass rose with an indicator for "North." Space for a compass rose is provided at the top of the game board.

Follow-Up

You may also want to connect a review session to this game by linking moves on the game board with correct responses to questions from the current social studies text lesson.

Direction March Cards

1 Space North	1 Space West
1 Space Northeast	1 Space Northwest
1 Space East	2 Spaces North
1 Space Southeast	2 Spaces Northeast
1 Space South	2 Spaces East
1 Space Southwest	2 Spaces Southeast

Direction March Cards (cont.)

2 Spaces South	3 Spaces East
2 Spaces Southwest	3 Spaces Southeast
2 Spaces West	3 Spaces South
2 Spaces Northwest	3 Spaces Southwest
3 Spaces North	3 Spaces South
3 Spaces Northeast	3 Spaces Northwest

Direction March Game Board

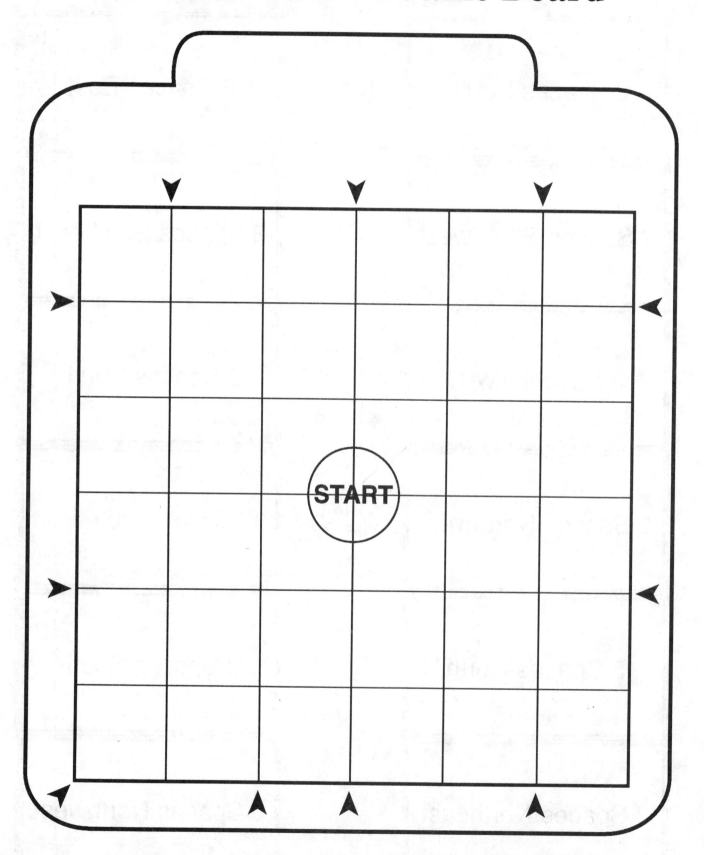

14

©1995 Teacher Created Materials, Inc.

A LEGEND-ary Masterpiece

Topic

Map legends (keys and symbols)

Objective

Students will devise map symbols for keys to accompany self-created maps of either real or imaginary places.

Materials

- 24" x 36" (61 cm x 91 cm) tagboard or cardboard (one piece for each group of students)
- various art supplies, from the traditional (crayons, markers, paints) to the creative (bottle caps, cotton balls, egg cartons, gravel, etc.)
- paint shirts or smocks for each student
- old newspapers to protect work surface
- old magazines

Preparation

Organize tagboard or art materials to make them accessible to students once they understand the project instructions.

Procedure

1. Put students into heterogeneous cooperative learning teams. Each team will make a large political and physical map of a real or imaginary place. If you are teaching a general unit on maps, a map of an imaginary place may be suitable; if you are studying a particular region of the world, students should make a map of an actual place.

2. Teams should incorporate a map key displaying symbols which represent important political features (cities, borders, canals, roads, railways, other man-made entities) and physical features (mountains, rivers, lakes, deserts, etc.) on the maps they create. Imaginary maps also need to be given titles that provide a clear idea of the area covered by the map. All maps must have a scale. Remind students that neatness and, for maps of actual places, accuracy are essential.

A LEGEND-ary Masterpiece *(cont.)*

Procedure *(cont.)*

3. Encourage students to be creative in devising symbols for their keys, for example, using blue ribbon to represent rivers or cotton balls streaked with brown paint to represent swamps. Give students just enough guidance to get their creative juices flowing in order to create their "masterpieces."

Background

"A LEGEND-ary Masterpiece" uses a whole-brain approach to map skills: reading map symbols is a left-brained skill; creating map symbols is a right-brained skill. Using both sides of the brain may help students remember the meaning of map symbols and the use of keys.

Since this project makes a good display of student work, you may wish to have students participate in this simulation prior to an open house or parent conferences.

Follow-Up

Each student team can hide its completed map key with construction paper, then exchange maps with another team. They then would try to identify the major symbols of each other's legends. The same activity could be done with the whole class, with each team's map being discussed by all. Each student team could also write problems to solve using the map scale they created. To facilitate this follow-up, mount the maps on a bulletin board.

For another slant on "A LEGEND-ary Masterpiece," have students use actual weather maps as a basis for designing alternatives to the standard meteorological symbols.

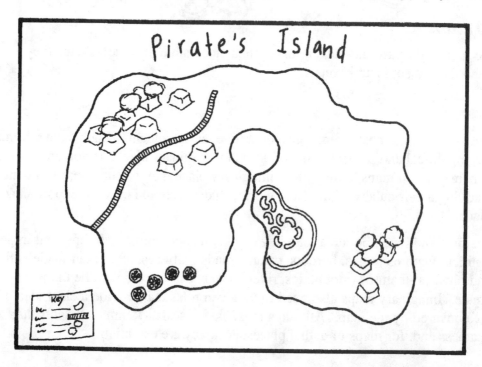

Up Periscope

Topic

Employing skills to identify latitude and longitude

Objective

Students will identify specific places on a map by giving latitude and longitude coordinates.

Materials

- a map of a particular region under study which has lines of latitude and longitude labeled, reproduced (one copy for each student plus two additional copies)
- overhead transparencies of the same map (two copies)
- an overhead projector

Preparation

1. Reproduce copies of the map.
2. Take two copies of the map and place an "X" within a coordinate grid square formed by the lines of latitude and longitude anywhere upon the map. Mark a different spot on each map.
3. Make two overhead transparencies of an unmarked map (one for each team involved).

Procedure

1. Divide the class into two teams.
2. After distributing copies of the map to each student, select a "periscope operator" for each team. Give each "operator" an X-marked map and tell them that the X on their map is the secret target for the opposing team; the opposing team has a similar map with a different secret target marked. The operator's role is to plot proposed target locations as offered by his or her teammates.
3. On a rotating basis, each operator will use the transparency of the map on the overhead to entertain latitude/longitude coordinate guesses from his or her team. Each member of the team is given the opportunity to offer an estimated coordinate location. If the guess does not fall within the coordinate grid square of the marked target on the operator's map, the operator places an "N" on the missed coordinate on the overhead transparency. If it does fall somewhere on the targeted grid square, the operator places "Y" on that spot. **Note:** Remind students to present the latitudinal coordinate first and the longitudinal one second, and to include the proper directional number of degrees north, south, east, or west.

Up Periscope (cont.)

Procedure (cont.)

4. All four corners of the marked grid square must be identified for the target to be declared "captured." Once the initial corner of the grid square has been identified, a team is in a position to deduce the remaining three corners of the target. The first team to name all four corners of the targeted grid square is the winner.

Background

This is an excellent activity for giving students practice using latitude and longitude. The simulated race to be first to identify the secret target is quite compelling for most classes.

Follow-Up

This activity also may be applied to highway road maps that use a letter and number grid. The local automobile club is usually an excellent source of highway road maps.

Another way to play "Up Periscope" would be to have multiple targets on specific sites. Give a team a specific clue and have them give the latitude and longitude coordinates for that site. For example, if South America were being studied, a clue might be, "This is the oldest capital city in South America." Students would then have to offer the coordinates

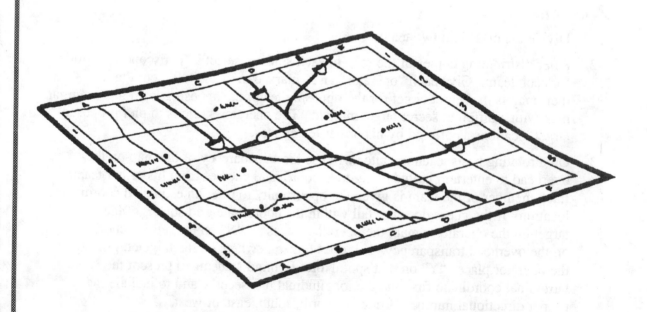

Sample Overhead Transparency Map

An "X" has been placed at the four corners of the designated unseen target. It is displayed here for demonstration purposes.

0 Equator

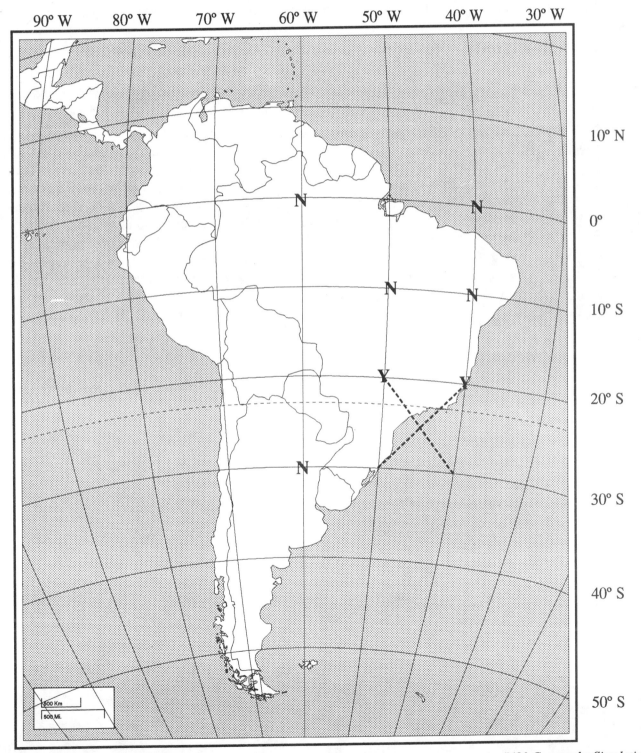

Cumulative Geography

SIMULATION #5

Topic
Using graphs

Objective
Students will correctly retrieve information from geography-related graphs.

Materials
- overhead transparencies of page 22 and/or 23
- an overhead projector

Preparation

1. Make transparencies of one or both graphs and, using a washable pen, fill in the graphs with six pieces of related data. (Page 22 is designed to be the basis of a vertical bar or line graph; page 23 is designed to be the basis of a horizontal bar or line graph.) The types of data you choose are completely up to you, but might include, for example, the size of the world's six oceans, the six most populated states in the United States, the six poorest nations in the world on a per capita basis, etc. (**Note:** You may also use already prepared graph worksheets that accompany your social studies text for this activity.)

2. Obtain and ready an overhead projector.

Procedure

1. After teaching a skills unit pertaining to graphs, divide the class into heterogeneous cooperative learning teams.

2. Place one of the prepared graph transparencies on the overhead projector and ask the first team a question with an answer that is about an item on the graph, but about which data is not found on the graph itself. For example, if the transparency displays data regarding the length of the world's six longest rivers, you might ask the team which of the rivers listed is located in South America.

    If the team answers that the correct river is, in this case, the Amazon, they would be given the opportunity to gain points by correctly identifying the length of the Amazon by reading the information on the graph.

3. Continue in the same manner with the rest of the teams.

Cumulative Geography *(cont.)*

Procedure *(cont.)*

4. Score is kept by using the figure associated with the correctly guessed graph answer. Using the same example, the team that correctly guessed the Amazon would receive a score of approximately 4,100 points, which is equivalent to the length in miles of the river.

   You may wish to reinforce graphing skills by asking student teams to make their own graphs representing the teams' cumulative points totals. A sample is provided at the bottom of this page.

5. Play ends after a set number of questions has been asked of each team. The team with the highest cumulative point total wins.

Background

Graphing is another dry skill for students. "Cumulative Geography" sparks interest by introducing competition during a final review of a graph skills unit.

Sample Graph

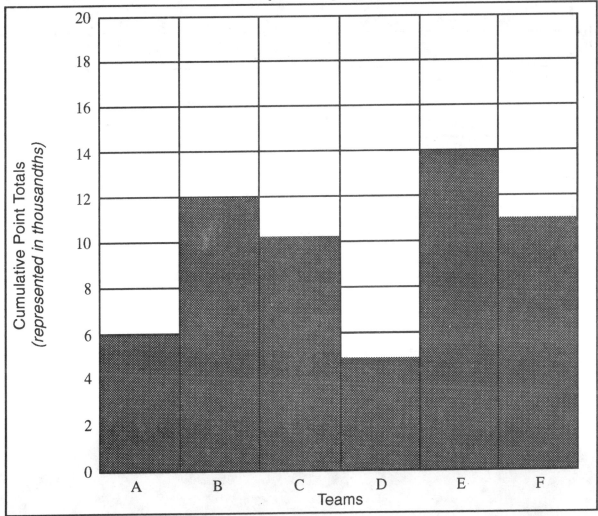

Graph I (Vertical)

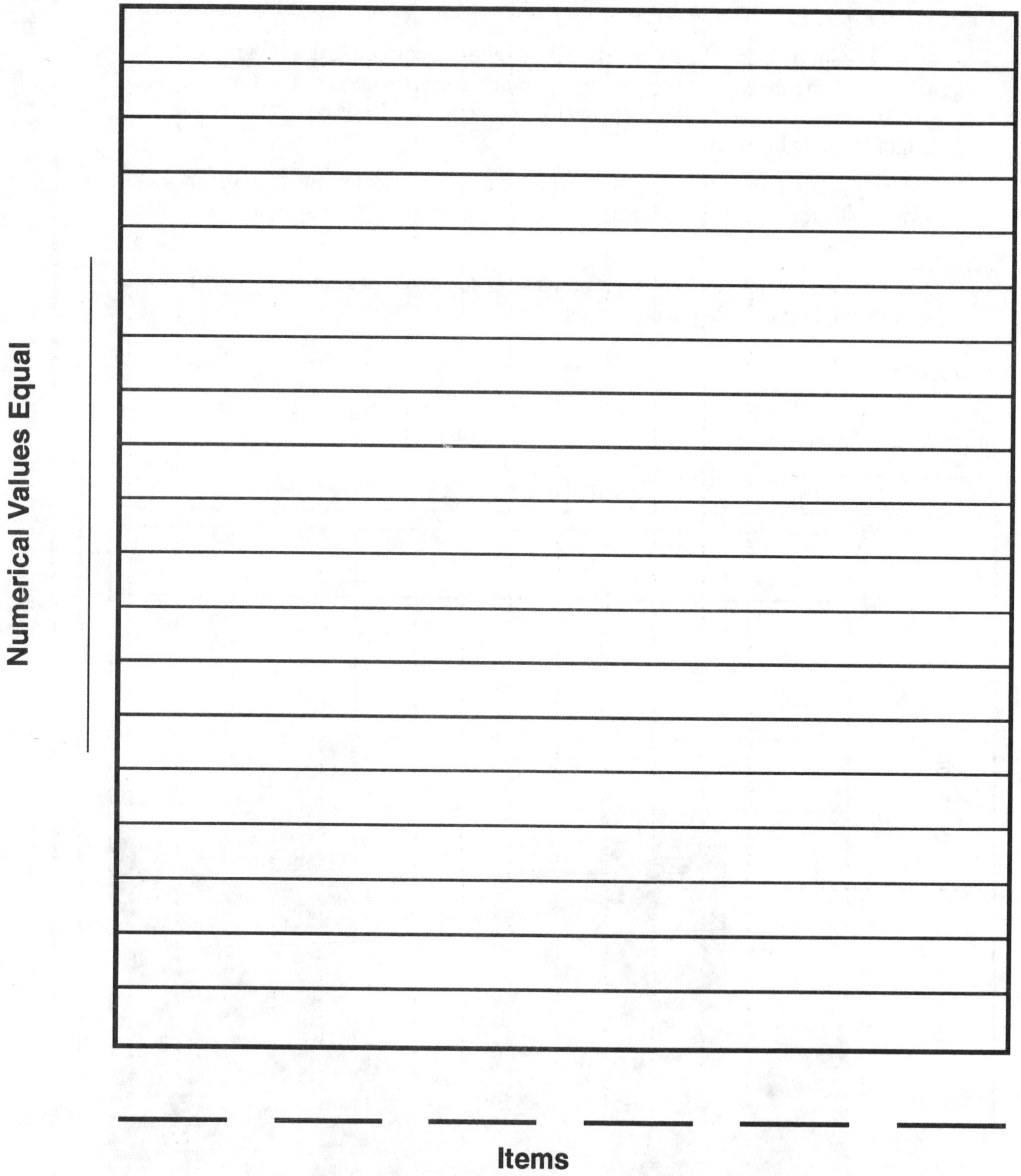

Numerical Values Equal

Items

Graph II (Horizontal)

Items

Numerical Values Equal

_____

Bus Stop

SIMULATION #6

Topic

Using map scale to find distance between locations

Objective

Students will use map scale to locate the geographic feature closest to a specific capital city.

Materials

- a continental map depicting both physical and political features of the area under study (one copy or textbook for each student)
- a selection from pages 26–31 appropriate for the area under study (one copy)
- rulers with both standard and metric measure for each student

Preparation

1. Copy, cut out, and shuffle the selected "Bus Stop" tickets.
2. Make copies of the continental map if a textbook map is not being used.

Procedure

1. Divide students into heterogeneous cooperative learning teams of four members each.
2. Direct each team to choose a capital city in one of the countries in the continental region under study. No two teams should choose the same city.

Bus Stop *(cont.)*

Procedure *(cont.)*

3. Explain that the capital city they have chosen is to be their desired destination on a simulated bus tour. However, the bus does not necessarily go directly to their city. The object of the simulated bus trip is for students to guess when the bus has come as close as it will get to their city. Be sure to tell the students how many bus stops there will be on their trip so that teams can determine the odds of getting closer to their chosen capital with each successive stop. (There are sixteen tickets on each page; you may add additional stops on similarly sized slips of paper if you wish.)

4. Draw a ticket from the top of the stack and announce the location of the first bus stop. Give teams an appropriate amount of time (1–2 minutes) to use map scale to determine the distance between the feature or site you announced and their capital cities. Teams of four may split into two pairs to determine distance during the first minute and to cross-check each pair's accuracy during the second minute.

5. Continue drawing tickets and announcing bus stops. When a team believes the stated feature or site is as close as the bus will get to their chosen capital city, one member of the team should call out, "Driver, stop!" You may want to record the team number and the distance between the stop and the city on the chalkboard each time a team calls its final stop.

6. When all teams have chosen a stop, or when all features or sites have been announced, the team with the least distance between its chosen capital and the stop where they "disembarked" is declared the winner.

Background

"Bus Stop" is a lively activity that can be used to practice using a map scale as well as to provide a comprehensive review of major geographic features within a region.

Bus Stop Tickets for Africa

Destination	
Lake Victoria	**Southern tip of Algeria**
Mt. Kilimanjaro	**Northern tip of Chad**
Mouth of the Zaire (Congo) River	**Easternmost tip of mainland Africa**
Cape of Good Hope	**Alexandria, Egypt**
Source of the Niger River	**Johannesburg, South Africa**
Victoria Falls	**Strait of Gibraltar**
Mouth of the Zambezi River	**Southern coast of Ghana**
Lake Chad	**Confluence of the Blue and White Nile**

Bus Stop Tickets for Asia

Destination	**Mt. Everest**	Destination	**Northern tip of the Philippines**
Destination	**Lake Baikal**	Destination	**Bombay, India**
Destination	**Mouth of the Ganges River**	Destination	**Mouth of the Yangtze River**
Destination	**Hong Kong**	Destination	**Calcutta, India**
Destination	**Easternmost tip of India**	Destination	**Canton, China**
Destination	**Southern tip of Japan**	Destination	**Karachi, Pakistan**
Destination	**Western tip of Indonesia**	Destination	**Shanghai, China**
Destination	**Aral Sea**	Destination	**Vladivostok, Russia**

Bus Stop Tickets for Europe

Destination	**Mt. Blanc**

Destination	**Northern shore of the Adriatic Sea**

Destination	**Barcelona, Spain**

Destination	**Munich, Germany**

Destination	**Southern tip of the Iberian Peninsula**

Destination	**Western tip of Crete**

Destination	**Shetland Islands**

Destination	**Mt. Elbrus**

Destination	**St. Petersburg (Leningrad), Russia**

Destination	**Mouth of the Rhine River**

Destination	**Hamburg, Germany**

Destination	**Strait of Gibraltar**

Destination	**Northern tip of Corsica**

Destination	**Source of the Danube River**

Destination	**Marseille, France**

Destination	**Mouth of the Loire River**

Bus Stop Tickets for Middle East

Destination	Destination
Sea of Marmara	**Istanbul, Turkey**
Mt. Ararat	**Western tip of the "Neutral Zone"**
Source of the Euphrates River	**Mecca, Saudi Arabia**
Shatt Al Arat	**Mosul, Iraq**
Strait of Hormuz	**Nile River Delta**
Southern tip of Sinai Peninsula	**Northeast corner of Syria**
Dead Sea	**Mt. Damavand**
Southwest corner of Oman	**Suez Canal**

Bus Stop Tickets for North America

Destination	**Southern tip of Greenland**
Destination	**Monterrey, Mexico**
Destination	**Anchorage, Alaska**
Destination	**Edmonton, Canada**
Destination	**Vancouver Island**
Destination	**Mouth of the Rio Grande River**
Destination	**Chicago, Illinois**
Destination	**Mt. McKinley**
Destination	**Southern tip of Florida**
Destination	**Mt. Whitney**
Destination	**Panama Canal**
Destination	**Mt. Citlaltepetl**
Destination	**South shore of Lake Erie**
Destination	**Mouth of the Mississippi River**
Destination	**Los Angeles, California**
Destination	**Source of the Missouri River**

30 *©1995 Teacher Created Materials, Inc.*

Bus Stop Tickets for South America

Destination	Destination
Lake Maracaibo	**Mouth of the Rio De La Plata River**
Mt. Aconcagua	**Galapagos Islands**
Northern edge of the Atacama Desert	**Falkland Islands**
Cape Horn	**Sao Paulo, Brazil**
Mouth of the Amazon River	**Punta Arenas, Chile**
Strait of Magellan	**Island of Trinidad**
Northernmost point of Brazil	**Southernmost tip of Columbia**
Lake Titicaca	**Easternmost tip of Brazil**

Georummy

Topic

Major political/physical features of a continent or world region

Objective

Students will identify the major nations or states, capital cities, mountains, deserts, rivers, swampland, and other bodies of water associated with a continent or world region under study.

Materials

- a list (as determined by the teacher) of the major physical and political features of a continent or region under study
- pages 34–35 (enough copies to create Georummy cards equal to the number of items on the features list)
- an overhead projector (optional)

Preparation

1. Prepare a list of political and physical features. For example, if Europe is being studied, any or all of its 30 nations and their capitals could be listed. The list could also include major rivers, mountains, bodies of water (seas, lakes, oceans), swamplands, etc.

2. Make enough copies of the appropriate Georummy feature cards to match your list. (**Note:** An optional blank card is provided for teachers who wish to add additional features to the seven listed in the objective.)

3. Write a specific place name for each feature on the center line of the appropriate Georummy card. For example, Madrid would be placed on a capital card, the Alps on a mountain card, etc. Responsible students with neat printing may do this step for you.

   For durable future use, laminate each of the cards.

4. Obtain and ready an overhead projector, if desired.

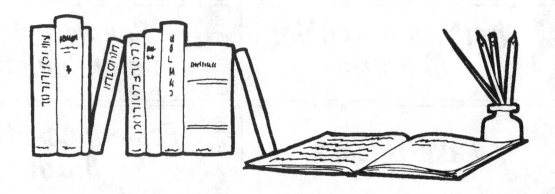

Georummy *(cont.)*

Procedure

1. "Georummy," a geographically oriented version of rummy, may be played by small groups of 2–4 students or with larger heterogeneous cooperative learning teams. If you choose the latter, shuffle the cards and deal six to each team. Start a discard pile by leaving one card face up.

2. As in traditional rummy, teams (players) attempt to get three or more cards displaying the same kind of geographic feature. To provide smoother play for an entire class, the teacher may use an overhead projector to list the cards currently in the discard pile. Teams selecting cards from the discard pile must pick up all the cards, beginning with the card they wish to take.

3. Play stops with the first team to rid itself of all cards in its hand by matching three or more of a kind or via discard. Points are totaled by adding the values indicated at the bottom of each card. Instructors may wish to score only points gathered by the first team to go out, or to add a penalty for picking up a large discard pile by also scoring the negative totals of the remaining teams.

4. Continue playing as many hands as time permits.

Background

"Georummy" is another flexible learning activity to familiarize students with the world around them. It can be used as an anticipatory set before introducing a region or as a review activity. It can also be at a learning center where pupils may play quietly during free time.

A variation of "Georummy" can be played by combining decks of cards for four or more continents or regions. This would also provide an additional score for matching three or more features from the same continent or region.

SIMULATION #7

Georummy Feature Cards

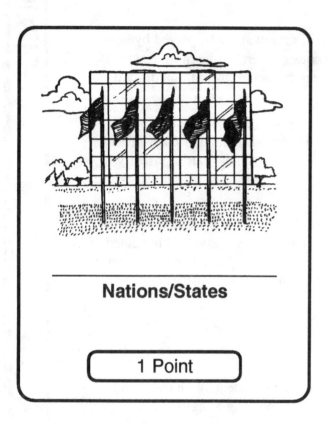

Nations/States

1 Point

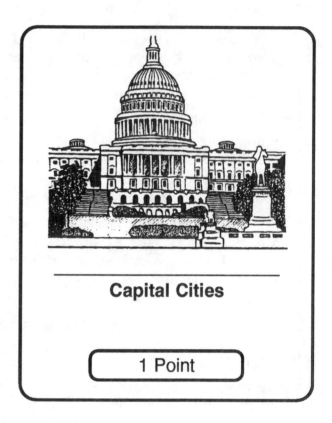

Capital Cities

1 Point

Rivers

2 Points

Mountain Ranges and Peaks

3 Points

Georummy Feature Cards *(cont.)*

Lakes, Seas, Oceans

3 Points

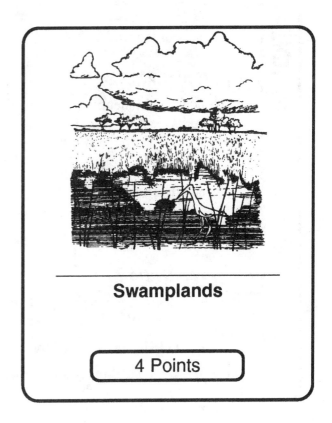

Swamplands

4 Points

Deserts

5 Points

_____ Points

SIMULATION #8

River Cruise

Topic

Rivers of the world

Objective

Students will identify major rivers of the world by the location of their sources, their mouths, and/or other significant details of their courses.

Materials

- an overhead projector
- pages 38–39 (one copy of each page)
- overhead transparency of page 40

Preparation

1. Reproduce copies of the clue sheets and cut out the individual river cruise tickets. Keep related cards together but place them in random order.

2. Prepare an overhead transparency of the River Cruise game board.

3. Obtain and ready an overhead projector.

Procedure

1. Divide the class into heterogeneous cooperative learning teams.

2. Tell students that they will be playing a game that allows review of the major rivers of the world. You will read a clue about a famous river, and each team in turn will try to identify its name.

3. There are three levels of play during each game, determined by the degree of difficulty involved in identifying that particular set of rivers by its clues. The levels are "Still Water" (easy), "Swift Current" (average), and "White Water Rapids" (challenging). For each level of play, the teacher presents the overhead transparency of the game board with six unknown rivers labeled A, B, C, D, E, and F, corresponding to the labels on the cruise tickets. There are four clues for each of the six rivers.

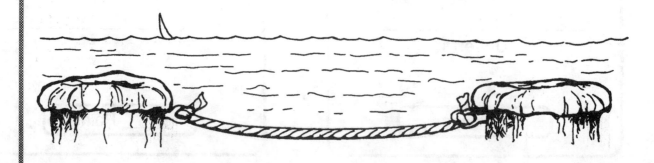

River Cruise *(cont.)*

Procedure *(cont.)*

4. Teams orally choose a clue for any of the six rivers by calling out a letter A–F. During the "Still Water" level of play, a river identified on the first clue given is worth 40 points. Guessing the name of a river correctly on the second clue garners 30 points; on the third clue, 20 points; and on the fourth clue, 10 points. The point values change with each level of play.

5. Note that tickets for the Still Water Cruise (easy level) have already been provided. You may wish to prepare additional sets of four clues each for Swift Current (average) and White Water Rapids (challenging) levels. (Some teachers may involve student teams in researching and developing the clues.) Simply block out the clues on an existing set of tickets and reproduce blank tickets for the next level of difficulty. The new clues may be written directly onto the blank tickets.

6. Play continues until all the rivers for a level have been identified, or all clues have been used. (**Note:** One, two, or all three levels of play may constitute a game.) The team with the greatest number of points is the winner.

Background

"River Cruise" not only reviews information about rivers, it invites students to tune their listening skills as clues are read aloud only once. You may encourage team members to take notes in order to maintain possession of clues throughout the competition.

On the game board, space is provided for checking off each clue given for a river. When the river is identified, circle the appropriate point value and record the name of the team which first recognized it. When changing levels, leave the circled scores for each river at the previous level of play, noting the team that garnered the points. Erase the clue number notations and team record in order to initiate a different level of play.

Still Water Cruise Tickets

Mississippi River Cruise (A)
a. Its source is Lake Itasca in Minnesota.

Mississippi River Cruise (A)
b. Its basin reaches from the Rockies to the Appalachians.

Mississippi River Cruise (A)
c. The Native Americans called it the "Father of Waters."

Mississippi River Cruise (A)
d. Its mouth empties into the Gulf of Mexico.

Missouri River Cruise (B)
a. Its source is in the Northern Rockies of the United States.

Missouri River Cruise (B)
b. Lewis and Clark followed it in exploring the Louisiana Purchase.

Missouri River Cruise (B)
c. It forms the border between Iowa and Nebraska.

Missouri River Cruise (B)
d. Its mouth empties into a larger river at St. Louis, Missouri.

Rio Grande River Cruise (C)
a. Its source is in the Rockies of Southern Colorado.

Rio Grande River Cruise (C)
b. It flows south-southeast.

Rio Grande River Cruise (C)
c. It forms the border of Mexico and the United States.

Rio Grande River Cruise (C)
d. It empties into the Gulf of Mexico.

Still Water Cruise Tickets *(cont.)*

Colorado River Cruise (D)

a. It flows southwest from its source in the Colorado Rockies.

Colorado River Cruise (D)

b. It carved the Grand Canyon.

Colorado River Cruise (D)

c. Its water is used by several states and two nations for irrigation.

Colorado River Cruise (D)

d. Its mouth opens into the Gulf of California.

Amazon River Cruise (E)

a. Its source is in the Andes Mountains of Eastern Peru.

Amazon River Cruise (E)

b. It flows eastward close to the equator.

Amazon River Cruise (E)

c. It has the largest volume of water of any river in the world.

Amazon River Cruise (E)

d. It empties into the Atlantic Ocean on the east coast of South America.

Nile River Cruise (F)

a. From its source in the highlands of East Africa, it flows northward.

Nile River Cruise (F)

b. It has a "Blue" and a "White" tributary.

Nile River Cruise (F)

c. It loses half of its water through evaporation in the Sudd.

Nile River Cruise (F)

d. Its mouth has a large delta and empties into the Mediterranean Sea.

River Cruise Game Board

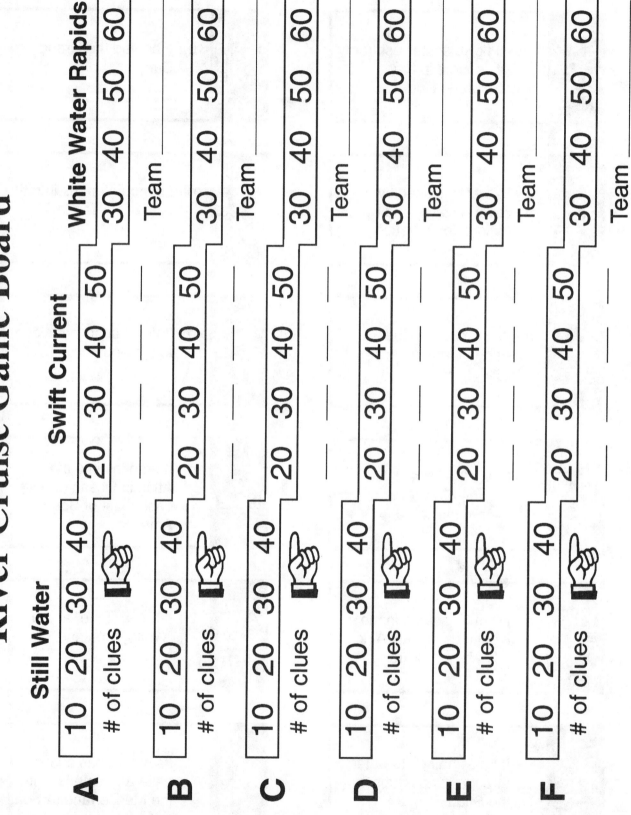

Still Water   **Swift Current**   **White Water Rapids**

A
10 20 30 40   20 30 40 50   30 40 50 60
# of clues — — — —   Team _____

B
10 20 30 40   20 30 40 50   30 40 50 60
# of clues — — — —   Team _____

C
10 20 30 40   20 30 40 50   30 40 50 60
# of clues — — — —   Team _____

D
10 20 30 40   20 30 40 50   30 40 50 60
# of clues — — — —   Team _____

E
10 20 30 40   20 30 40 50   30 40 50 60
# of clues — — — —   Team _____

F
10 20 30 40   20 30 40 50   30 40 50 60
# of clues — — — —   Team _____

Mission: Iraq

Topic

Iraq or any other nation of major interest in current events

Objective

Students will research pertinent information dealing with the geography of Iraq or other nation using a variety of resources. They will then make a graphic display of the data on a student-made map of the country.

Materials

- a large piece of tagboard for each student team
- reference resources: encyclopedias, almanacs, atlases, current news magazines, newspapers, etc.
- page 42 (one copy for each student team)
- a reward or reinforcer for the winning team (See page 94 for ideas.)

Preparation

1. Write in the name of the nation under study, the due date, and your name as the "President's Representative" in the appropriate blanks on a copy of page 42.

2. Make copies of the completed page 42 for the student teams.

Procedure

1. Divide the class into heterogeneous cooperative learning teams.

2. Give a copy of page 42 to each team. Orally review it with students as they read silently.

Background

While this learning activity grew out of the public's interest in Iraq during Operation Desert Storm, you may substitute any nation prominent in current events. On page 42, the slant on a nation's war capabilities may be replaced by a study of its economic strengths.

Research, map skills, and teamwork are stressed in this activity. Those students utilizing the most references will receive the reward you determine to be appropriate.

Follow-Up

An amusing way to introduce this activity is to dress as a spy, using props such as a trench coat, sunglasses, magnifying glass, etc. Don't discount such theatrics; an enthusiastic introduction sets an upbeat, positive tone for the project.

Mission:_____

Here is the project for your Mission Force:_____

Using any map(s) you can locate in your reference resources, make an accurate physical/political map of _____ on the provided sheet of paper.

Since you are our government's top "intelligence team," you will need to locate all the important locales within _____ and find out what these places offer to our government.

For example, locate the areas that produce important products that might need to sustain a war—steel factories, chemical plants, oil refineries, production of food stuffs, etc. If these types of products are unavailable in _____, find out from which nations it imports such goods or weapons in order to wage war.

Use current, up-to-date encyclopedias, newspaper articles, news magazines, atlases, and world almanacs to obtain the most recent information on _____. Be sure to keep an accurate list of the sources you use to turn in with your finished map.

Completed missions will be scored as follows: One point will be awarded for each piece of factual information displayed on your map concerning the geography, land use, products, natural resources, military installations, and imports of _____. The most effective briefing on _____ resources (which will be given by the team with the most points) will be personally rewarded by the President's Representative, _____, in this class.

Remember! Your government is counting on you to gather as much accurate information on _____ as possible and have it neatly displayed on your map by this date:_____.

Yum-Yum Trees

SIMULATION #10

Topic

Human integration with the environment: conservation of resources

Objective

Students will devise at least one possible solution to the problem-solving dilemma presented in the activity. They will name at least three renewable and three nonrenewable natural resources that are subjects of contemporary conservation measures.

Materials

- pages 45–46 (one copy for each student)

Preparation

Make an appropriate number of copies of pages 45–46.

Procedure

1. Divide the class into heterogeneous cooperative learning teams. Ask each team to choose a reporter or spokesperson.

2. Pass out copies of pages 45–46 to each student. Orally review the dilemma with the students as they read silently to themselves.

3. Have teams convene in a brainstorming session for three to five minutes. All possible ideas for solving the dilemma are presented by team members without censorship.

4. During a subsequent three– to five–minute session, teams should begin to eliminate those solutions with unfavorable consequences for the Ube tribe. Using general consensus, each team should settle upon what they believe to be their single best solution to share with the class.

5. Each spokesperson should share his or her team's solution with the class and field questions from classmates and/or the instructor. Any idea should be accepted if there is evidence of critical thinking in the team's decision-making process.

SIMULATION #10

Yum-Yum Trees *(cont.)*

For Discussion

After all teams have shared their suggestions, conduct a discussion regarding the question of what might have caused the extinction of the Ube's yum-yums. While some students may suggest natural causes for the extinction of the yum-yum trees, others will undoubtedly bring up the point that the tribe over-harvested the trees without regard to eventual consequences. Make a connection between this observation and similar damage which has occurred in the world's present environment. Other questions to ask might include, What possible cost did the Ubes face because of an error in conservation? Are there any lessons in the dilemma of the Ubes that pertain to society today?

Next, discuss the meaning of "renewable" and "nonrenewable" natural resources. Give some examples of each to stimulate thought, then have teams or individual students make a list of renewable and/or nonrenewable resources that are the subject of conservation measures in the local, national, or global community.

Background

This problem-solving activity presents several topics for investigation. While there are no definite right or wrong answers for this dilemma, certain solutions have more potential than others. For example, the Ubes may decide that it's better to send small bands of people to obtain yum-yums, or that seeds might be brought back from the excursion instead of entire trees. However, all student-generated solutions should be considered. Whatever solutions are generated, be sure to use the activity to discuss not only how geography determines how people live, but how contemporary people have risked their future by showing an uncontrollable appetite for natural resources.

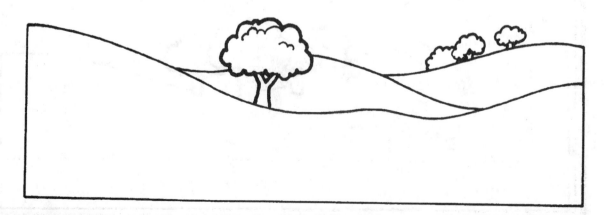

The Yum-Yum Tree Dilemma

For many years, the peaceable Ube tribe used the wood from yum-yum trees to make canoes and build huts in their village. They also used the fruit from the yum-yum tree in their cooking. Eventually, the Ubes used up all the yum-yums trees around the village. The Ubes would have to go elsewhere to obtain their favorite tree, but where?

The tribe finally heard that there were some yum-yum trees located atop Chimney Cliffs. The only trouble was, the cliffs dropped a sheer 200 feet (60m) to the Deepwet Ocean. Chimney Cliffs and the yum-yum trees that grew there were many days away by canoe. In addition, a vicious headhunting tribe, the Onos, patrolled the stormy waters of the Deepwet Ocean near the Ube village, making travel by sea difficult.

To complicate matters, the Ubes were also surrounded by formidable natural barriers that made travel by land difficult as well. By foot, a round trip across the Hot Pepper Desert would take almost a month. The Raging River was too swift to navigate upstream. And the Snowy Mountains were so high they were impassable.

But even with all the obstacles, the Ubes still felt that they must have yum-yum trees. Using the accompanying map and some problem solving, make a plan that the Ube tribe can use to get more yum-yum trees.

Questions to Consider

- Should the Ubes try to collect wood and harvest fruit from the yum-yums above Chimney Cliffs to take to their village?

- Should the whole Ube tribe consider migrating to the area rich with yum-yum trees?

- Is there a way to return the Ube village to its former state of having plentiful yum-yum trees? If they can restore the yum-yum tree population, how can they avoid a recurrence of the same situation?

- Is war with the Onos a possibility? If so, would victory for the Ubes solve their basic problem? Why? Why not?

Yum-Yum Territory Map

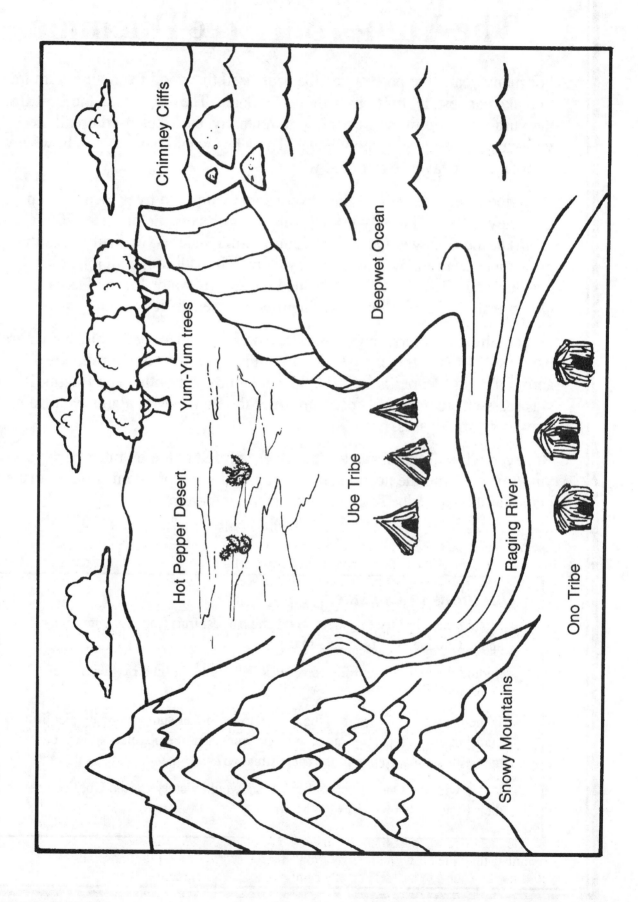

46

©*1995 Teacher Created Materials, Inc.*

Green Thumb

Topic

The effect of climatic regions upon agricultural production

Objective

Students will match various crops to the climatic region where they can be grown.

Materials

- page 49
- a list of crops by climatic region (See page 48.)
- 18" x 24" (46 cm x 61 cm) sheets of tagboard (one for each team)
- overhead projector (optional)

Preparation

1. Make enough copies of the climatic cards so that the total number of cards equals three times the number of cooperative learning teams in the class. You may wish to ask student volunteers to cut apart the cards.

2. Write the list of crops by climatic region on poster board or on an overhead transparency.

3. Obtain and ready an overhead projector if the list is on a transparency.

Procedure

1. Divide the class into heterogeneous cooperative learning teams.

2. Explain that during the next period of study (a week or more), each team will simulate the establishment of a successful farming industry. Ask each team to draw a 3" (8 cm) grid on the tagboard, creating a total of 48 squares. Each square will represent 100 acres (40 hectares) of tillable soil.

3. Shuffle the cards from page 49, then deal three cards to each student team.

4. Explain that each time a team (or team member) correctly answers a question from a specific lesson, the team can choose from the posted list a crop which will grow under the climatic conditions designated on their cards. One hundred acres, i.e., a grid square, of that crop is then cultivated on the team's "farm."

5. Students may write in the name, use a color code, or create a symbol of their selected crops to fill in grid squares. Since agricultural diversity is encouraged, no single type of crop may take up more than 500 acres (200 hectares). If students choose the crop "vegetables," they may vary the type of vegetable they would like to cultivate, i.e., carrots and celery, but they may not have more than 500 acres total of vegetables.

6. On a regular basis, check the progress of each team's farm. Crops must correspond to the climatic condition cards; should they not, the misplaced crops will be stricken from the farm due to "pestilence," "disease," or other "natural disasters." Remember that a team with an "irrigation" card may grow crops that normally would not be found in a desert or other unfavorable environment.

SIMULATION #11

Green Thumb (cont.)

Procedure (cont.)

7. At the end of the prescribed time period, the team with the greatest acreage under successful cultivation is declared the winner.

Background

"Green Thumb" may be limited to the social studies period, but it can also be used as a sponge activity throughout the day. Ongoing research by students is encouraged so that they avoid misplacing crops. Any crop is acceptable as long as it fits one of the climatic conditions on their cards.

The student-created farms will demonstrate the effects that the existence of the two or three climatic regions within a nation may have on its agricultural industry. Just as there are nations with poor climates for growing food, some teams may find they have been dealt poor cards and will have little opportunity to cultivate their acreage.

The following is a partial list of the crops available in each type of climatic region:

Equatorial	**Mediterranean**	**Humid Continental**
coconuts	olives	vegetables
bananas	grapes	potatoes
rice	citrus fruits	corn
teak	fig	wheat
mahogany	wheat*	soybeans
	vegetables*	oats
		orchards

Marine	**Humid Subtropical**	**Mountain**
wheat	cotton	tea
sugar beets	rice	coffee
orchards	sugar cane	cotton
vegetables	tea	
corn	peanuts	
rye	vegetables	
	citrus fruits	

Savanna	**Semidesert**	**Desert**
corn	vegetables*	vegetables*
millet	citrus fruits	citrus fruit*
beans		
wheat		

*These crops may be grown in this region only if there is irrigation.

Green Thumb Climate Cards

Equatorial
(Tropical)

Hot and wet year round

Marine
Ocean-dominated climate with warm, moist summers and cool, generally wet winters

Savanna
(Tropical, wet, and dry)

Hot with alternate seasons of wet and dry conditions

Humid Continental
Characteristic of interior regions of continents; warm to hot summers and cold to extremely cold winters; precipitation varies

Desert
(Arid)

Extremely limited precipitation with temperatures varying from hot to cold depending upon time of day or night

Humid Subtropical
Hot summers, warm winters; precipitation year round in the form of rain

Semidesert
(Semi-arid)

Limited precipitation, often with great range in temperatures

Mountain
Varies from place to place depending upon latitude and altitude

Mediterranean
Hot, dry summers; cool, wet winters

Subarctic
Characteristic of the high latitudes; cool, short summers; long, extremely cold winters; moderate precipitation, mostly snow

Irrigation

One Person's Bread, Another Person's Poison

Topic

The consequences of asbestos use, a hazardous natural resource

Objective

Students will become aware of the economic, social, and health ramifications of asbestos use after its dangers became known.

Materials

- pages 52–53 (one copy for each student)

Preparation

Make copies of pages 52–53.

Procedure

1. Divide students into heterogeneous cooperative learning teams of four.

2. Hand out pages 52–53 and review them orally while students read along silently.

3. Within their teams, have students discuss the following questions.

> ## Questions to Consider:
>
> Although John and Bill are totally unknown to each other, how are their lives related?
>
> Which man faces the more difficult dilemma?
>
> Can you see any hope for either man?
>
> Which man is responsible for his fate?
>
> How is geography related to each man's life?

Depending upon time limitations, teams may also share their ideas with each other before you conduct a whole class discussion. One way to encourage cross-discussion is to have teams exchange spokespersons to be interviewed for their team's views.

One Person's Bread, Another Person's Poison *(cont.)*

For Discussion

To get team members involved in discussion, have the teams assign one spokesperson for each question. Call upon the spokespeople to share their group's ideas. This gets all the ideas on the table at once. Students may then respond with any opposing points of view.

An important additional question should be presented during the whole class discussion: Are there any other widely used natural resources known to be health hazards?

While there is a large list of hazardous substances ranging from mercury to uranium, most are probably unknown to students. One probable exception is tobacco. A major agricultural and industrial force in several southeastern states, tobacco companies frequently make the news with regard to their product's direct link to cancer and heart disease. To make the connection between asbestos and tobacco for the students, ask them what the effect would be if a court ruled that a tobacco company was directly liable for the death of a cancer patient.

Background

"One Person's Bread, Another Person's Poison" is a critical thinking activity designed to show the double-edged sword natural resources can be. Students most likely will not solve the dilemma, nor should a solution be expected. However, they should be made aware of the types of problems people struggle with when they are confronted with the complex integration of geography, economics, and individual welfare.

John's Story

John sat listlessly in front of the television. Another day was passing by, another day without work. In one more week his unemployment benefits would run out, and then he and his family's only lifeline of support would have to be some form of government-sponsored welfare.

Ever since the asbestos mine drastically reduced its work force six months ago, John had been looking steadfastly for other work. With determination at first, he had investigated job possibilities at the rate of two per day for several weeks. However, the longer he remained unemployed, the fewer job opportunities he found, and none of the jobs offered the pay and benefits equal to those from his work as a miner. Besides, with so many unemployed workers to pick from, the best new jobs were snatched by younger people who appeared to be sharper than 45-year-old John. The best chance to find work would be to move his family over 200 miles away. However, it would take money to move a family and relocate, and the harsh reality was that John had little money left.

At a time when John should have been at his peak, he was faced with the possible loss of his home, his car, and his dignity. He was in utter despair.

Bill's Story

Bill sat in the doctor's office in a complete state of shock. The nagging cough he had come to see the doctor about several weeks ago was supposed to be nothing more than a mild case of bronchitis, wasn't it? Having never smoked, he never in his wildest imagination believed he could have lung cancer. Lung cancer! The words struck him more powerfully than a 20-pound sledge hammer.

While gathering his wits about him, Bill heard the doctor mentioning something about work-related conditions, something about asbestos fibers. Bill's 20 years of experience in the construction business passed through his mind like a slide show. Early in his career he had worked often with asbestos roofing material. Later, he worked on fire-proofing heat ducts and insulating electrical wiring with asbestos. Always there were the brittle particles that flew up into the air like bits of pollen. And then, during recent years, the use of asbestos had been severely reduced and workers had begun using elaborate safety precautions when it was present.

Again Bill became conscious of the doctor's voice: "There's a 30 percent chance of living a normal life expectancy, 70 percent chance of surviving only five more years."

At age 45, Bill's life, though not yet over, had become blanketed by a very deep, dark cloud of uncertainty.

Cramped Quarters

SIMULATION #13

Topic

How the large Japanese population has adapted to its limited area of land

Objective

Students will use courtesy and any other methods or organizational tactics needed to function in limited space for a portion of a school day. They will list at least two ways the Japanese have adapted their life styles to the restricted space within their nation.

Materials

- masking tape
- teacher-selected reward or incentive, optional (See page 94 for ideas.)

Preparation

Use masking tape on the floor to section off a portion of the classroom before students arrive. Desks may also be moved into this reduced classroom area.

Procedure

1. Divide the class into heterogeneous cooperative learning teams.

2. Restrict the students from seating themselves in the manner normally used for teams. Instead, move the student groups to the designated portion of the room.

3. You may wish to fabricate an excuse for such an arrangement, such as wanting to bring in a large display table, or you may be straight-forward, telling students that you'd like to see how they would react if their regular work space was significantly reduced.

4. Encourage students to be particular mindful of others under the reduced space conditions. Everyone will be cramped, so courtesy will be appreciated. Common phrases such as "Excuse me," "You may go first," and "May I pass through here?" will become mandatory in keeping students from becoming annoyed with one another.

5. If you have some type of reinforcement plan in place, you may wish to award bonus points to groups whose individuals express the most consideration toward members of both their own and other groups.

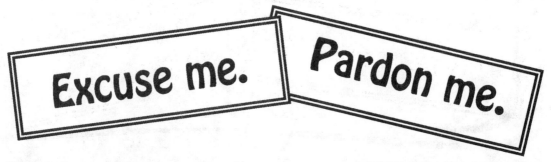

Cramped Quarters *(cont.)*

Procedure *(cont.)*

6. You may allow student teams time to brainstorm ways that they could best handle the tight environment. For example, they may decide to cooperate with adjacent groups by assigning monitors to obtain supplies, sharpen pencils, etc., or they may change the order in which groups leave their seats to line up to leave the classroom. Many other creative ideas may be devised to facilitate classroom management during this activity.

7. Some students may not easily adjust to the change in environment. For this reason, plan to keep this arrangement in place for no more than a single period or day.

For Discussion

Be sure to debrief students before the day or period is over. Have them imagine what it would be like to spend a daily portion of one's life under such congested conditions. At this point introduce the facts concerning the population density of Japan (see the "Background" section). Then ask, What are some methods the Japanese have developed to cope with their limited space? Are there any occasions in our own country when crowded conditions may cause us to alter our behavior in a positive way to adjust to those conditions? What advantages does being polite offer under crowded conditions?

Background

With a population more than half that of the United States and a total land area less than the state of California, Japan has faced severe space shortages throughout their history, but have adapted well to space limitations. For example, they build small houses with sliding interior panels that can be used to create a single spacious room from two smaller ones. Their home landscaping may even include miniature plants known as bonsai.

Presently, an apartment in a prime Tokyo locale may cost more than a million dollars. With restricted opportunities to purchase real estate at home, many Japanese businesses have invested in foreign properties. Among the Japanese, Hawaii has become a favorite location in which to purchase vacation property. When premium-priced Hawaiian real estate looks like a bargain, it gives some idea of how expensive, and precious, land is in Japan.

You may go first.

May I pass through here?

SIMULATION #14

Leftovers

Topic

Subsistence farming

Objective

Students will identify subsistence farmers as those who generally work unwanted land and grow only enough food for the immediate needs of their families.

Materials

- a box of cornflakes
- a box of cereal that includes a variety of tasty morsels or trail mix that includes chocolate bits
- paper cups (one for each student)
- small slips of paper
- transparency of page 58

Preparation

1. Before class begins, fill approximately 10–20% of the paper cups with the tastier cereal or trail mix.

2. Fill the remaining cups only half full with cornflakes. To really play up the point of this simulation, decrease the amount of cereal in the final four or five cups.

Procedure

1. Pass out the slips of paper. Then have the students number off and write down their numbers onto the slips.

2. Tell the class that you have brought in some cereal for them to eat today. However, since all the food is not all the same, you will randomly draw numbers to determine the order in which it will be distributed.

3. Call out a number at random. The person whose number is called first may select whichever cup of cereal he or she wishes. Continue this procedure until all the students have cups of plain or tasty cereal.

For Discussion

After the last of the food has been distributed, display the "Discussion/Analysis Chart" (page 58) on an overhead projector. Complete the chart together as you ask students to respond to the questions on page 57.

Leftovers *(cont.)*

For Discussion (cont.)

> ### *Questions to Consider:*
>
> How many of you got something you really enjoyed?
>
> How many of you had a full cup?
>
> How many of you had more than one type of item in your cup?
>
> Of those who had a full cup of many items, how many of you gave some away or traded with someone else?
>
> How many of you feel you were short-changed?

Encourage those students who felt short-changed to share their thoughts on their bad fortune. Then point out that when there are only limited resources of value, not everyone can get the best ingredients; hence, the random draw.

Finally, have them imagine that the cereal cups represent their daily food portions. Ask students to respond to the discussion questions at the bottom of page 58.

Background

Subsistence farming is a wide spread agricultural practice found throughout much of the underdeveloped Third World nations and even in some developed regions. Many people in Latin America, Africa, and Asia derive their entire living from cultivating marginally productive soil to grow just enough for their family's needs. For these farmers, there is no surplus to barter or sell for cash in order to improve their lot in life. In some cases, the best land in a region has been staked out for commercial agriculture and peasants must rely on the land that is "left over."

While "Leftovers" could be used after the introduction of subsistence farming to the class, the full impact of this simulation is greater when it is used as an anticipatory set. Unless you regularly provide food in the classroom, this lesson will cause students to think about the circumstances that engendered such unexpected generosity—or inequity—when the simulation is presented prior to a unit on farming.

Finally, many students will find fault with the lack of fairness in this activity, but it is important to note that subsistence farming is not always viewed as inequitable. While in some regions, like Latin America, large land holdings have been the focus of reform efforts and even revolutions. In many parts of the world, subsistence farming is not so much a question of equity as it is survival, as large populations attempt to grow food on limited land resources.

Discussion/Analysis Chart

Question	No. of Students	Comments
How many of you got something you really enjoyed?		
How many of you had a full cup?		
How many of you had more than one type of item in your cup?		
Of those who had a full cup of many items, how many of you gave some away or traded with someone else?		
How many of you feel you were short-changed?		

For Further Discussion

Imagine that the cereal cups represent their daily food portions.

What might your diet be like?

Would it be full and varied, or meager and limited in choice?

Apple Market

Topic

The economies of various world regions

Objective

Students will use various reference materials to research economic diversity within a region. Students will identify several major economic resources (products, natural resources, etc.) of a particular region and identify at least one affluent nation and one impoverished nation within that region.

Materials

- a variety of reference materials (encyclopedias, atlases, almanacs, etc.)
- a variety of "white elephant" items (supplied by students)
- several bright red apples or other edible treats
- copies of page 62

Preparation

1. Make several copies of the play money on page 62 and cut it apart. (Student volunteers may do this task.)

2. Write the names of the nations within the region under study on slips of paper to be drawn by student teams. The number of nations should equal the number of student teams that will be created.

3. Obtain the apples or other treats.

Procedure

1. This activity will take approximately three class periods. During the first period, team the students in pairs. Pass around a bowl or hat containing slips of paper and have teams draw out the names of the nations that they will study.

2. Tell the teams that they are to research the per capita income (PCI) of their nation to get an idea of the nation's relative wealth within the region. PCI is the average annual amount of income made by each individual within that nation, though in some countries, PCI is skewed when a small segment of the population controls most of the material wealth. Still, PCI provides a basis for comparing the wealth of one nation to another within a region. A table of selected nations from the Middle East and their PCI is shown on page 60 for exemplary purposes; the figures can also be found in almanacs. The teams should also research the major exports of their nations to find out which natural resources or products are abundant.

Apple Market *(cont.)*

Procedure *(cont.)*

Nation	PCI (with date)	Nation	PCI (with date)
Bahrain	$7,300 (1989)	Iraq	$1,950 (1989)
Kuwait	$6,200 (1991)	Egypt	$720 (1991)
Yemen	$545 (1990)	Lebanon	$1,400 (1991)
United Arab Emirates	$12,100 (1989)	Saudi Arabia	$5,800 (1991)

3. The PCI information will be used to operate an auction-like activity of the white elephants brought in by the students for the second class period of this simulation. (**Note:** Be sure to tell students that they should get their parents' permission before bringing any household items to school.)

4. Funds for the auction are allocated as follows: For every $100 PCI, each team is given one dollar in Apple Market Funds (AMF). For example, the team representing the United Arab Emirates would receive 121 AMF, while the team representing Egypt would receive only 7 AMF. Round off the PCI to the nearest hundred dollars to determine the exact number of AMF each country should receive.

5. A team can earn additional AMF by selling products. However, a nation's PCI dictates what it can or cannot sell because each team may bring in only one item for every $500 of PCI they have. Using the same nations in this example, the team representing the United Arab Emirates would be eligible to bring in 24 items, but the team representing Egypt would be allowed to bring in only one. The exception to this would be any items closely associated to the chief exports of the team's nation's chief exports. Therefore, if lumber and paper products are major exports, pencils and any paper products would be permitted for auction.

Apple Market *(cont.)*

Procedure *(cont.)*

6. In random order, each student team will auction its items, exchanging the appropriate amount of AMF per item in each transaction.

7. The last, unannounced element to add to this simulation are the edible items you yourself bring to the auction. These items should be auctioned to the highest bidders. This means that at the end of the auction, only teams that used their economic resources wisely will be able to purchase these premium items.

For Discussion

In the third class period for this activity, students should be placed in larger, heterogeneous cooperative learning teams to tackle these questions: How do poor nations fare in economic competition with their wealthier neighbors? How can nations with limited natural resources compete with their surrounding countries with more resources? Can a nation with little natural resource wealth use other means to make itself prosper? Has disparity in wealth ever led to open conflict between two nations?

Background

Played over three days, Apple Market is a stimulating way to introduce your students to the economic reality of various regions of our contemporary world. Students are able to contrast the economic welfare of nations throughout one region and in subsequent regions as the year progresses.

Throughout history, economic competition has been a basis of conflict. For example, Japan's involvement in World War II was predicated upon its need to secure natural resources for its expanding industries. Today, Japan is a model of success for resource-poor nations, having harnessed the power of its mightiest resource—its people.

Apple Market Funds

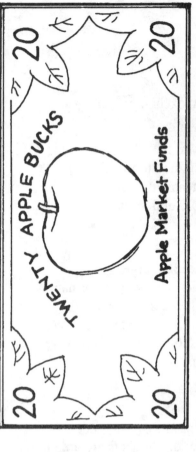

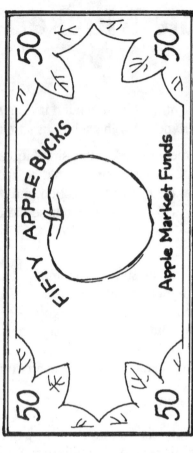

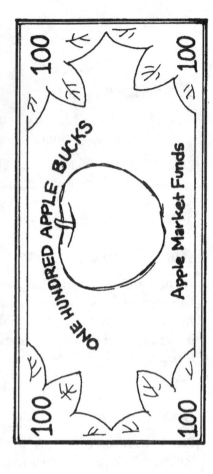

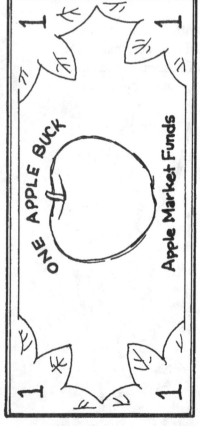

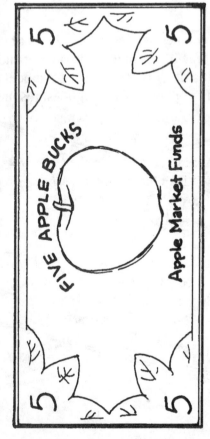

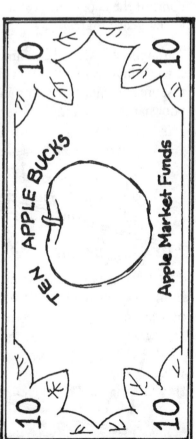

62

©*1995 Teacher Created Materials, Inc.*

The Import Collection

Topic
Imported goods in the American economy

Objective
Students will gain awareness of the prevalence of imported goods in their daily lives. They will define the terms "import" and "global economy."

Materials
- a large bulletin board
- a world map for the bulletin board
- labels or packaging from imported goods that include the point of origin, i.e., canned fish, clothing, toys, etc.
- yarn (optional)

Preparation
Gather the materials and begin preparing bulletin board space for this project.

Procedure
1. Center the world map on the bulletin board and attach the various product labels or packages so that they are aligned with the nation of origin. You may wish to use yarn to connect the product with its home. Then use the bulletin board to introduce the class to the concept of imports.

2. Ask students to bring in product labels from imported goods that they use at home. (**Note:** Be sure students have parents' permission to bring in the items.)

3. Student-supplied labels should be added to the bulletin board (See sample map on page 64.). To integrate math and map skills, keep a record showing the distances that the products had to travel.

For Discussion
This activity may be as short in duration as a week or continued for several months. Either way, as the bulletin board becomes filled with labels, focus the students' attention on the emerging economic picture it depicts. Do most products come from one particular region? Can types of products from a particular region be categorized in any way? If so, what does this information tell us about the way people in that region make a living? What types of products are in greatest representation overall? What is a global economy? How is it depicted in this display?

The Import Collection *(cont.)*

Background

"Think globally" is a phrase in vogue these days, especially in business. For most adults, the world seems to have "shrunk" due to advances in communication, mass media, and industrial technology.

But as adults marvel, for example, at the number of products required from other nations to manufacture one automobile, students are often unaware of the impact foreign business has on their lives. While most know that many cars and electronics come from Japan, they might be surprised to learn that the all-American hamburger stand sells apple juice from Canada and uses toys from China in its promotions. They may also be amazed to discover that discount chains touting American products also sell clothing manufactured in places like Sri Lanka, Bangladesh, and Honduras. Hopefully, this simulation will awaken an awareness that in the future the competition for a high standard of living may be international in scope.

Sample Bulletin Board

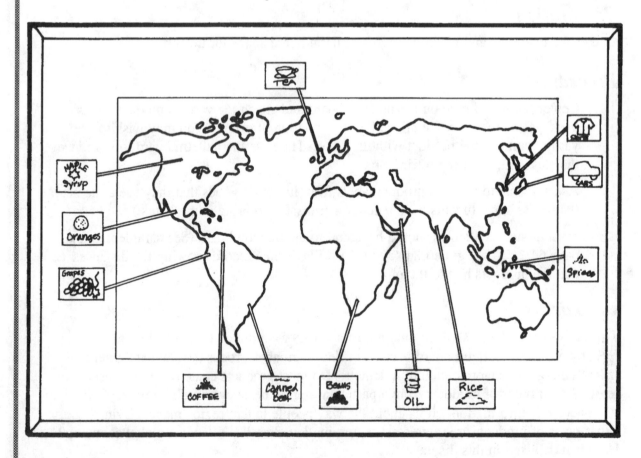

Symbolic Resources

Topic

Natural resources of a geographic region

Objective

Students will name the major natural resources of a specific geographic region as a part of a review of other pertinent geographic information.

Materials

- textbook lesson on the geography of a specific world region
- resource-related "prizes" (See page 94 for ideas.)

Preparation

Procure enough prizes to provide for your largest student group.

Procedure

1. Divide the class into heterogeneous cooperative learning teams.

2. After beginning a chapter or unit on the geography of a particular world region, hold a random drawing to assign one nation from that region to each student team.

3. Allocate class time for teams to research the major natural resources of their nation. They may use the textbook or other reference material. You should examine each team's list of natural resources, verifying it according to the team's references.

4. Have each team make an identifying symbol for its country which incorporates a map, a national flag, or an emblem. These symbols will identify the team's nation in the review game.

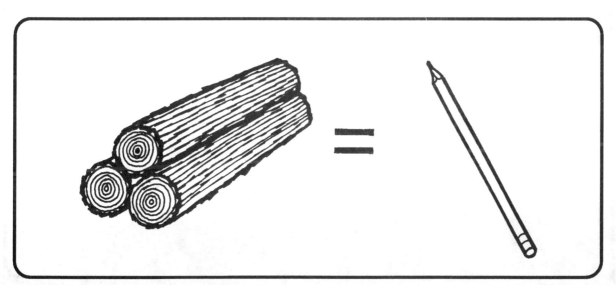

SIMULATION #17

Symbolic Resources *(cont.)*

Procedure *(cont.)*

5. When the chapter or unit about the region nears closure, review its major objectives with the following game:

    *   On the chalkboard or overhead projector, display a comprehensive list of the natural resources of the region.

    *   Call upon each team in turn to answer a review question dealing with the geography of the region. If the team answers correctly, they may select one of its major resources from the presented list. Be certain to verify that the chosen resource is, indeed, one of the resources of that nation.

    *   If the team has, in fact, correctly chosen a resource, the team receives a "prize" symbolic of that resource. (The list on page 67 should give you a foundation for building a list of resources and symbolic prizes.)

    *   No score is kept. Whether or not a question is answered correctly will determine the distribution of prizes. The game ends after a specified question or time limit has been reached.

Background

The draw of this game for students is the suspense of what type of prize the team may receive. As you look over the list on page 67, you will notice that some prizes are, in fact, "duds," such as the prize of aluminum foil for the resource of bauxite.

Such prizes will be eschewed, while others, such as a chocolate bar for the resource of cacao, will be coveted. Not knowing what prize will turn up next will keep the students riveted on the review activity and make them eager to respond correctly to the questions.

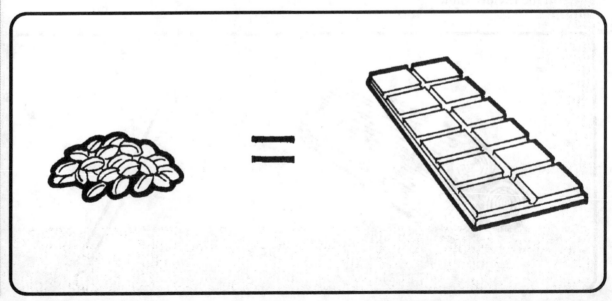

Symbolic Resources (cont.)

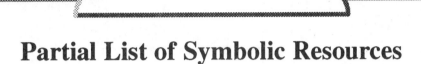

Partial List of Symbolic Resources

Bauxite: Aluminum Foil

Cacao: Chocolate Bar

Chicle: Chewing Gum

Chromium: Paper Clips

Coal: Coal Lumps

Coffee: Coffee Beans

Corn: Cornflakes, Popcorn

Cotton: Cotton Balls

Fish: Fish-shaped Crackers

Fertilizer: Dry Cat Food

Fruit: Samples of Fruit

Iron: Paper Clips

Livestock: Plastic Livestock Models

Oil: Scrap Plastic

Peanuts: Peanuts

Potatoes: Potato Chips

Rice: Rice Cereal

Rubber: Erasers

Rye: Rye Bread

Sugar Cane: Sugar Cubes

Tea: Tea Bags

Tin: Tin Cans

Tobacco: Loose Tobacco

Wheat: Crackers

Temps, Inc.

Topic

Temporary migration within Europe and/or North America

Objective

Students will give one reason for temporary migration.

Materials

- a series of review questions regarding European or North American geography
- reward for the winning team (optional; see page 94 for suggestions)

Preparation

Prepare review questions.

Procedure

1. Divide students into heterogeneous cooperative learning teams and number the teams consecutively.

2. Explain that the teams will be participating in a review game that will demonstrate the concept of temporary migration as had been discussed during the unit. The winning team may receive an award.

3. Each team is to select one member from the team numbered ahead of them to be part of their group, i.e., Team 1 selects a member from Team 2, Team 2 from Team 3, and so on. The last team should select a member from Team 1.

4. Begin the game by asking questions of each team in turn, using whatever method of scoring you prefer.

5. When the game is over, instruct each team to determine its final score. Distribute a copy of page 70 to each team. Have teams use the steps outlined to first find a point value for each member of the team, including the student who was originally selected from a different team. That student now returns to his or her original team, taking points from the current team away and adding the points to the original team's total. For example, if Team 1 has four members and scores 100 points, 25 points are subtracted and the selected person takes those 25 points back to Team 2. Team 1 would gain any points that come with its returning member from the last team. In a close contest, the shift in points as team members "migrate" from group to group will have an effect on the final total points for all teams.

Temps, Inc. *(cont.)*

For Discussion

Depending upon the final outcome of this activity for each team, students may or may not be disturbed when some of their points are taken to another team. Discuss student reactions to this simulation and address the questions at the bottom of page 70.

Point out that the exercise which they just experienced simulates the conditions of temporary migration. Then begin a discussion using questions which address the causes of temporary migration such as, What is the purpose of temporary migration within a region? How might a host country benefit from an influx of temporary workers? How might it suffer?

Bring closure by pointing to the connection between the students' affective state with the ramifications of temporary migration, asking how workers, or people in general, in a host country might view temporary workers from other lands. Could there be potential problems between the two groups? In spite of problems, why would migratory workers come to the host country in the first place?

Background

Although examples of temporary migration may be found world-wide, Europe and North America have been chosen as focal points for this activity. Temporary migrants from southern Europe, including Turkey, have been commonplace in northern European cities since World War II.

Legally allowed to stay and work, these workers send a sizable amount of income back to families in their homelands and supply that nation with a significant portion of its national income. Although there was a need for cheap labor after the catastrophe of World War II, as lean economic times have increased job competition, resentment towards foreign workers has surfaced in Northern and Central Europe.

A similar scenario can be seen in parts of the United States, especially the Southwest, where thousands of migrant workers have crossed the Mexican border illegally to find better jobs. As in Europe, the newly arrived migrants send income to family members in their homelands, shifting the flow of American dollars to south of the border.

Scoring and Discussion Guide

Team Members _____

Total Points _____

How to Determine Your Team's Score

1. First find the point value (how many points each member receives). Divide the total points by the number of members in your team. Your team's point value is _____ .

2. The member from the other team receives this point value as well. However, he or she will leave your group and return (with his or her points) to the original group. You must subtract his or her point value from your total points to get your team's score.

   The team's score without the one member from the other group is

   _____ .

3. Now, add points from the team member who just returned to your group after being with another group. The team's score with your original member added in is _____. Is this score higher or lower than your first total?_____

Questions to Consider

- How do you feel about losing or gaining some points? Why do you feel that way?

- What do you think is the purpose of temporary migration within a region?

- How might a host country benefit from an influx of temporary workers? How might it suffer?

Economic Dominoes

Topic

The economic relationships between a land's natural resources and its potential industrial capabilities

Objective

Students will recognize that the relationships between various natural resources and industries affect the potential economic welfare of a nation. They will relate resources to their appropriate industrial use.

Materials

- copies of pages 74–77
- an overhead projector

Preparation

1. Use heavy paper to make copies of the "Economic Dominoes" on pages 74–77. Since the pages are different, try to divide their distribution evenly. For example, if there will be six teams, make three copies of each sheet. If there will be seven teams, four copies of one sheet and three of the other.

2. Laminate and cut out the dominoes. Shuffle them and then make random stacks consisting of 15 dominoes.

3. Before beginning the activity, copy the following list of natural resources, leaving off the category names. In addition, you may create the list either keeping the items in the order shown or putting them in random order, depending upon the ability level of your class. Display this list on the blackboard or on an overhead transparency.

arable soil	textiles	precious metals	vegetables
favorable climate	clothing	paper products	livestock
poor soil	chemicals		wool
arid climate	tools	corn	cotton
subarctic climate	smelting ores	wheat	timber and pulp
beautiful beaches	energy	rice	citrus
scenic mountains	tourism		bananas
	food processing	gold	coffee
tin		iron	sugar
copper	coal		tea
zinc	oil		fish
silver	natural gas		

$$\$\$\$\$\$\$\$\$\$\$\$ \; capital \; \$\$\$\$\$\$\$\$\$\$\$$$

Economic Dominoes *(cont.)*

Procedure

1. Use the list of resources to initiate a discussion. If you put the items in random order, ask students to categorize them by their characteristics. If the items were kept in the order shown, ask students to brainstorm possible classification titles.

2. Ask students if they can make any links between items in different categories and lead students to realize that products and industries can occur only with the right combination plus capital to finance its development. For instance, tourism will flourish with a favorable climate, beautiful beaches or scenic mountains. However, without the capital to build hotels, golf courses, etc., tourism will not prosper.

3. On the overhead, demonstrate the objective of Economic Dominoes, which is to create the greatest number of links between resources and industry. Similar to regular dominoes, the end of each Economic Domino must be related to an adjacent domino in order to form links. For example, agricultural resources must be linked to arable soil; industries must be linked to a source of capital and to a resource necessary to an industry. See below for examples of valid and invalid links.

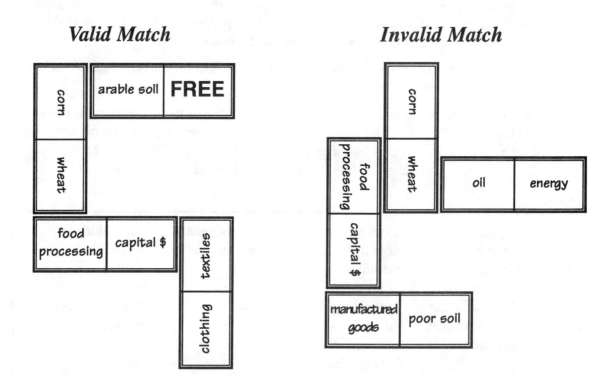

Valid Match

Invalid Match

4. Put students into heterogeneous cooperative learning teams and distribute one stack of 15 dominoes to each team. Instruct teams to link as many dominoes as possible from their assortment. The team connecting the most dominoes may be ruled the winner, or perhaps even better, declared an example of a very prosperous nation.

Economic Dominoes (*cont.*)

For Discussion

After allowing sufficient time for the domino activity, give teams an opportunity to share the "economies" they have created. This serves a dual purpose: you can validate correct links, and all the teams can discover how their economies compare with others.

Then ask the teams the following questions: If the dominoes represented the economy of a specific nation, how prosperous do you think this nation would be and why? What did your nation possess or lack that affected its success? A team which lacks capital might be asked how their economy could raise capital in order to develop industry.

Background

Some links will be stronger than others. Arable land and favorable climate may be matched with any resource, but poor soil, subarctic climates, and arid climates can be matched only with mineral resources. Scenic mountains and beautiful beaches could easily be directly attached to tourism, but the mountains may also be a source of mineral wealth.

Many links will be made using common sense. After all, coal is not directly tied to food processing, but a sharp group might link coal to energy and then link that with food processing. You may have to act as the final judge in such cases.

The most critical feature of Economic Dominoes is that, as in actual geography, resources and capital are limited. The economies that the teams construct will reflect various levels of national prosperity. Those teams without capital will be at a dead end in terms of industry, and their economy will be a reflection of a developing nation which exports resources and imports manufactured goods. But even teams with capital may not successfully connect all their dominoes, as they could lack resources to make more links. Their economy will be a reflection of a nation such as Japan, which has capital but must import needed resources.

Follow-Up

If time permits, perhaps some exporting and importing could be carried out, with teams trading extra capital for needed resources and vice versa. The "Economic Dominoes" of each group might change for better or worse after such transactions occur, providing more fuel for discussion.

Dominoes Cards

arable soil	**FREE**

poor soil	**FREE**

arable soil	**FREE**

poor soil	**FREE**

corn	wheat

zinc	silver

tin	favorable climate

rice	vegetables

precious metals industry	capital $

manufactured goods	poor soil

Dominoes Cards (cont.)

capital $	food processing

coffee	cotton

arid climate	poor soil

smelting ores	coal

copper	gold

iron	tools

clothing	textiles

chemical	oil

timber/pulp	subarctic climate

scenic mountains	wool

Dominoes Cards (cont.)

oil	energy	arable soil	livestock
beautiful beaches	tourism	food processing	capital $
timber/pulp	bananas	tea	arable soil
citrus	sugar	fish	arid climate
natural gas	energy	capital $	**FREE**

Dominoes Cards *(cont.)*

Directions: Write in the items of your choice on these blank dominoes.

Bilingual Lingo

Topic

Multilingual regions of the world

Objective

Students will identify a foreign word with clues gained by uncovering parts of a hidden international sign. Students will name one way in which multilingual regions have dealt with language barriers.

Materials

- an overhead projector
- transparencies of pages 80–85
- page 86 or a sheet of plain paper cut into odd shapes

Preparation

1. Make transparencies of the international signs from pages 80–85 that you wish to use.

2. Before class begins, place a transparency on the overhead and cover the sign and English translation of the foreign word with either the puzzle cover on page 86 or oddly-shaped pieces of plain paper reconstructed into its original shape. Number the cut pieces of paper.

Procedure

1. On the overhead, display only the foreign word or phrase and ask students if they know its meaning.

2. Then have students or teams randomly select a numbered shape to be removed from the illustration. The object is to see who will first decipher the meaning of the foreign phrase.

Bilingual Lingo *(cont.)*

Background

There are multilingual states and regions in many parts of the world. Throughout history, differences in language have been a factor in creating tensions between large groups of people co-existing in the same area. While one can point to Switzerland as an example of a country where four languages are spoken without creating problems, there are many more instances where language differences present significant communication barriers. For example, French-speaking Quebec has threatened secession from English-speaking Canada for several decades, in part because of language.

In some nations, like India, different languages and even different dialects within a language make a single national language impossible. And as post-communist Eastern Europe reshapes itself, various ethnic groups with distinct languages have tried to politically insulate themselves.

Western Europe, on the other hand, has successfully circumvented its language problems. Teaching English in schools, using the metric system for measurement, and employing international road signs has helped people and their respective governments adjust to living with "the people next door."

Follow-Up

Bilingual Lingo can be used as an interesting sponge activity when almost any topic is under review. As an added twist, link the removal of each puzzle piece to a correctly given answer to a review question.

International Sign

Service Station
Benzintank (Danish)

International Sign (cont.)

Pedestrians
Les Pietons (French)

International Sign *(cont.)*

Danger of Forest Fire
Pericolo D'Incendio (Italian)

 ©1995 Teacher Created Materials, Inc.

International Sign (cont.)

Soccer
Das Fussballspiel (German)

International Sign *(cont.)*

Volleyball
Voleibol (Spanish)

 ©*1995 Teacher Created Materials, Inc.*

International Sign (cont.)

Diving
Dykning (Swedish)

Puzzle Cover

Directions: Use this cover to hide international signs on the overhead.

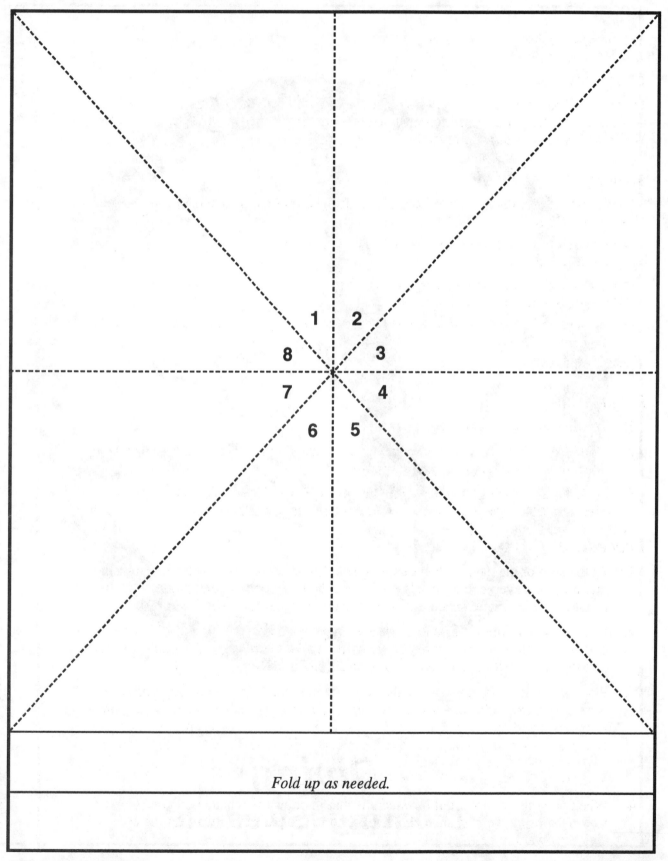

Fold up as needed.

86

©1995 Teacher Created Materials, Inc.

Muscovite Shopping

Topic

The collapse of Soviet communism

Objective

Students will identify one of the reasons for the downfall of communism as an inability to produce consumer goods. In addition, students will compare a map of the former Soviet Union with a map of the region after the collapse of Soviet communism.

Materials

- a container of used, worn pencils, in a quantity just enough to have only a small surplus after each student takes one
- a container of used, worn crayons, in the same quantity as the pencils
- assorted scrap paper
- shoe boxes or similarly sized containers for students so each may store writing implements and notebook paper
- newspaper and news magazine articles about life in Russia and other nations of the former Soviet Union
- maps on page 89

Preparation

1. Obtain pencils, crayons, and scrap paper.

2. Obtain shoe boxes. You may request that students supply their own boxes without offering an explanation for their purpose.

3. Seek out and invite individuals with ties to the Soviet Union to the classroom to offer anecdotes about the quality of life in that country, if possible.

Procedure

1. At the start of the day, explain that you have learned of a new organizational method that promises everyone in the class will become more efficient and productive. In fact, you are so excited about this new procedure you can't wait to start!

2. Have students store their pencils, crayons, and notebook paper in the designated containers. Be sure the containers are marked with their names and assure students that the items will be returned to them at the end of the day.

3. Place the containers of used pencils, crayons, and scrap paper in an appropriate central location. Tell students that whenever paper and pencil are needed, they are to form a line and take one pencil and/or crayon and one sheet of scrap paper from the designated supply. While you could dictate how lines should be formed, allowing students to form their own lines may be a better indicator of how students are reacting to the limited choice of supplies.

4. When crayons are used, tell the students that in order to exchange crayon colors they must bring their original choice back to the container and wait for the crayon they now want to be returned.

SIMULATION #21

Muscovite Shopping *(cont.)*

Procedure *(cont.)*

5. As the day progresses and each successive paper and pencil activity is completed, students likely will become restless and feel agitated about a system that seems so unproductive. Just remind them that there will be a class discussion at the end of the day about this matter. (See "For Discussion.")

6. In the afternoon—but not at the very end of the day—give a language arts assignment, asking students to express their thoughts about this new organizational system. Not surprisingly, many students will express feelings bordering on rebellion.

7. Return all collected supplies to each student before the end of the day.

For Discussion

During the last hour of the day, open discussion by having students share some of the ideas they wrote about the new distribution program. Did they view the system as being as productive as promised?

Without dwelling on the history of the Soviet Union, take a moment to draw on the conceptual relevance of the lesson. Ask them if they know why the former Soviet Union fell apart and why the communist government failed. Then illustrate the frustrations felt by the Soviets by using primary sources of information about everyday life under communism, using newspaper and magazine accounts describing the long lines for simple items such as bread, butter, and meat (if available); even worse, those at the end of the line often arrived at the front only to find the shelves barren of goods. The existence of a black market also points to the inefficiency of the communist market, where the government, not people's needs, prescribed what was to be produced.

Finally, ask students what stopped them from breaking order and using their confiscated supplies. They will more than likely concede that you, as the teacher, were still in charge.

Background

While the students experienced only a single day of frustration, the Soviets experienced over 70 years of frustration under their poorly devised economic system. Their misery caused them to face off against their own government's tanks in the streets of Moscow in August of 1991. Once the Soviet people had a small dose of freedom, they ignored the government control exerted over them for decades (centuries, if you consider the rule of the czars).

The Soviet breakup will not remain a major daily news event, but it will always be an example of how command economies ultimately fail. And, on a small scale, the pupils involved in this simulation will experience some empathy for their Soviet counterparts.

Extend the activity by having students compare the maps on page 89. Discuss the geographical changes that have taken place as a result of the collapse of Soviet communism.

Soviet Communism

Before the Collapse

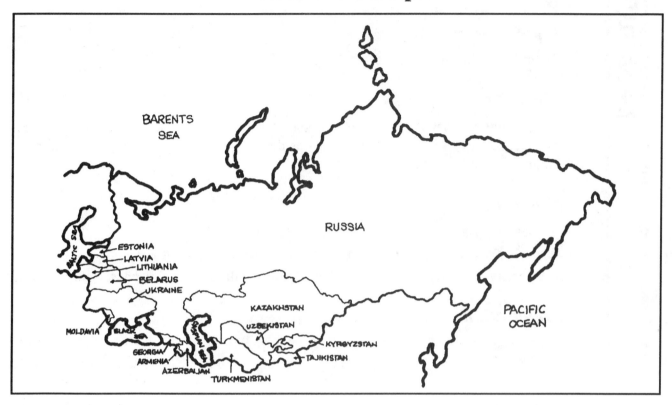

After the Collapse

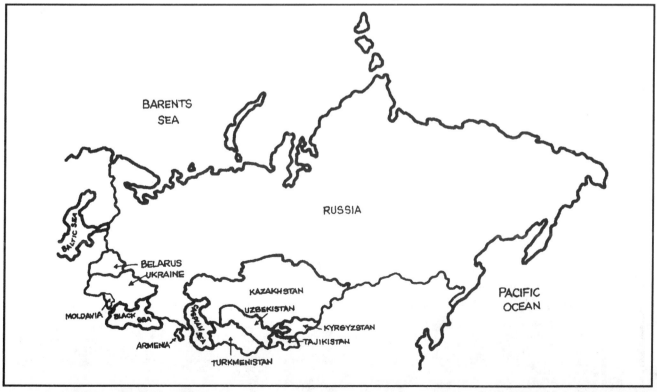

SIMULATION #22

Southeast Asian Exchange

Topic

General overview of Southeast Asia

Objective

Students will identify the major resources and/or exports of a specific nation in Southeast Asia. They will review other topics such as the region's history, geography, economy, and culture.

Materials

- copies of page 92 (about one dozen copies)
- teacher-created or textbook review questions about Southeast Asia
- a variety of reference materials (encyclopedias, atlases, and almanacs)

Preparation

1. Make copies of the exchange cards on page 92.
2. Create or locate in the textbook review questions about Southeast Asia.

Procedure

1. Divide the class into heterogeneous cooperative learning teams.

2. Assign a nation from Southeast Asia for each team to study. Using the reference materials, they are to locate the country's major natural resources and exports.

3. As teams work on their economic research, go through the resource material yourself, listing four major resources and/or exports of each country you assigned for study.

4. Total all the various resources and/or exports and then proceed to cut out an equal quantity of exchange cards so that there is one card for each item you listed.

5. Plan on a class period for an exchange review. Shuffle the Exchange cards you made and randomly distribute them so that each team has four cards.

6. Ask each team a review question in turn. If the team members answer correctly, allot them 30 seconds to trade one or more resources and/or exports. A designated team "barker" should call out which items his or her team is willing to trade and in what number, i.e., "We'd like to exchange two 'rubber cards.' What will your team give us?"

Southeast Asian Exchange *(cont.)*

Procedure *(cont.)*

7. At the end of either a pre-specified time or a question limit, the team with the highest dollar value of its own resources/exports is declared the winner, with each team using their research data to total their final dollar value. As each team announces its score, use your own list to verify the total of the highest scoring team.

Background

"Southeast Asian Exchange" incorporates research skills prior to review and at the same time gives students a chance to play the role of commodities traders.

Follow-Up

While the stated objective in the exchange is to recapture one's own resources and/or exports, the game could be reversed so that the goal would be the complete distribution of domestic resources and/or exports in order to attain the highest dollar value in return. To play this version, each team would start with four cards representing their own nation's major resources/exports.

Exchange Cards

RICE $10	**HEMP** $15	**TIN** $30
COTTON $15	**COCONUTS** $15	**RUBBER** $35
SPICES $15	**HARDWOODS** $20	**TEXTILES** $40
SUGAR $15	**COFFEE** $20	**ELECTRONICS** $50
BANANAS $15	**SILK** $25	**OIL** $60

©*1995 Teacher Created Materials, Inc.*

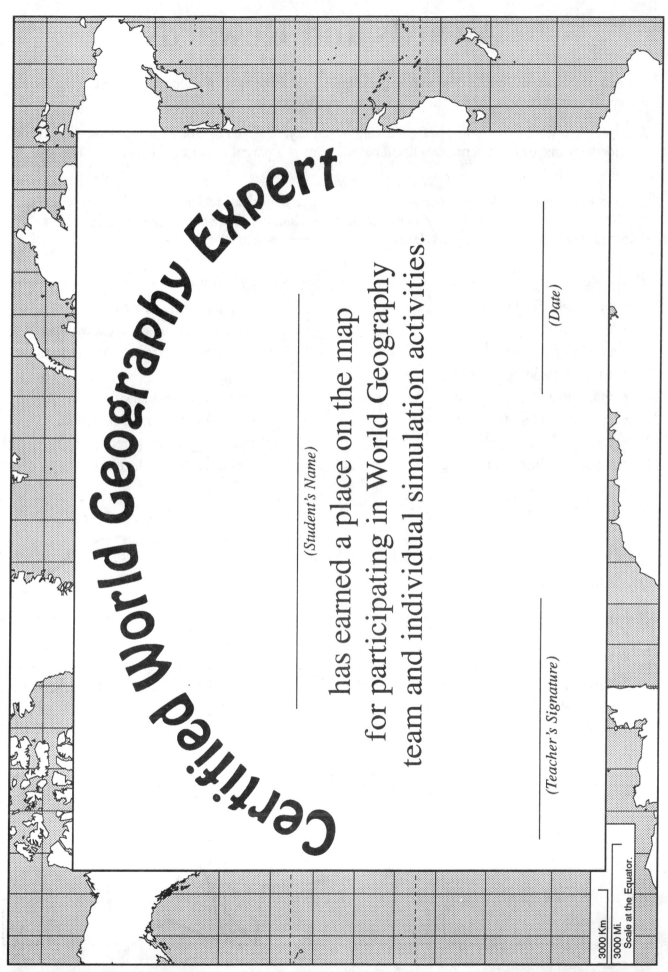

Certified World Geography Expert

(Student's Name)

has earned a place on the map
for participating in World Geography
team and individual simulation activities.

(Teacher's Signature)

(Date)

3000 Km
3000 Mi.
Scale at the Equator.

Awards and Rewards

Several of the simulations in this book suggest the use of some type of acknowledgment in the form of a positive reinforcement for success or cooperative effort during the activities.

If a specific reward is not stated in the simulation activity, or if you do not wish to use the suggestions provided, try one of the alternatives listed below. This is a partial list of the kinds of rewards you might decide to use.

Keep in mind that awards and rewards can fall into three major categories—recognition, privileges, and tangible rewards. No single kind of reinforcement works better than another. Select rewards for students, depending upon the grade level and/or the preferences of the students.

Privileges

- lunch with the teacher
- library pass
- computer use time
- pass for skipping homework
- tutor other students
- special "helper" for the day
- choice of some activity
- work on a special project, game, center, etc.

Recognition

- telephone call to parents
- name in class or school newspaper
- pat on the back for a job well done
- display work
- class cheer, chant, etc.
- student of the day, week, month
- note sent home to parents
- announcement to the class

Tangible Rewards

- popcorn party
- stickers
- bonus points or extra credit
- educational video or movie
- snack treats in the classroom
- grab bag or treasure chest
- hand stamp
- pencil, eraser, or other school supply
- tokens for no homework, extra recess, etc.

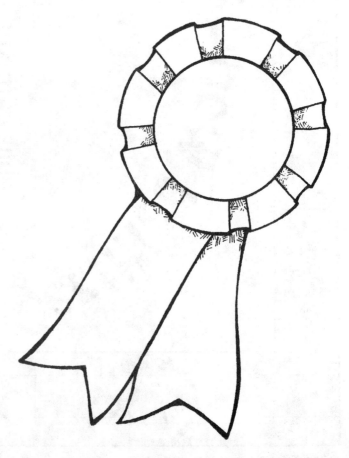

World Map

You may wish to use the map below as part of the extension tools for related cooperative team activities and simulations. Distribute copies to students as needed or prepare a transparency for use on the overhead projector.

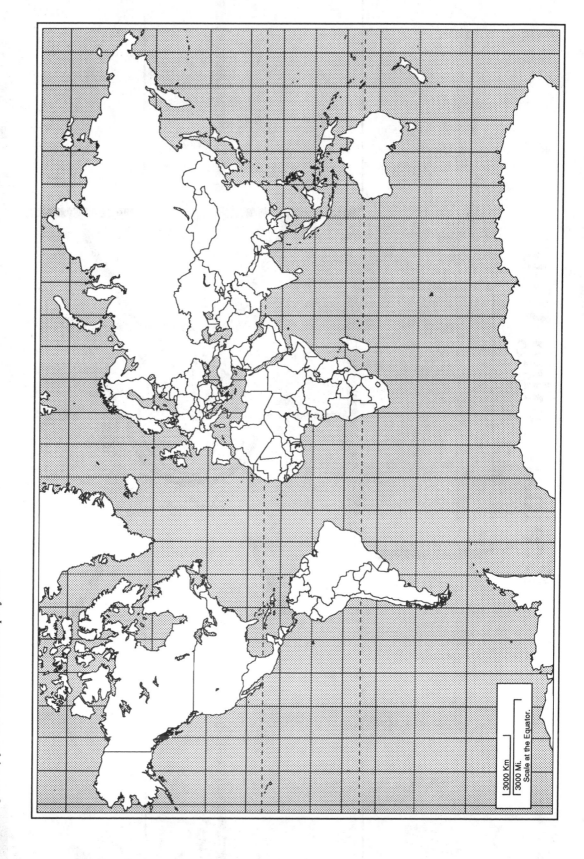

3000 Km
3000 Mi.
Scale at the Equator.

Brainstorming Web

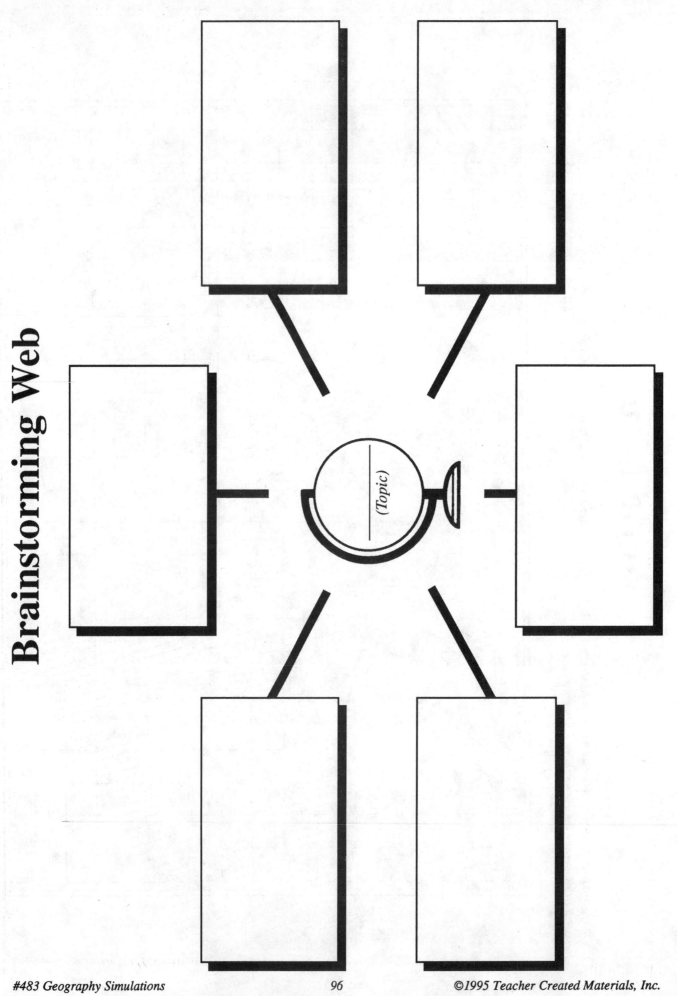

(Topic)

©1995 Teacher Created Materials, Inc.